DIASPORA BLUES

BOOKS BY CLIVE SINCLAIR

Novels
Bibliosexuality
Blood Libels

Stories
Hearts of Gold
Bedbugs

Literary Biography
The Brothers Singer

DIASPORA BLUES

A VIEW

OF

ISRAEL

Clive Sinclair

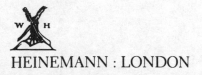

HEINEMANN : LONDON

William Heinemann Ltd
10 Upper Grosvenor Street, London W1X 9PA
LONDON MELBOURNE
JOHANNESBURG AUCKLAND

First published 1987

British Library Cataloguing in Publication Data

Sinclair, Clive, 1948–
    Diaspora blues : a view of Israel.
    1. Israel
    I. Title
    956.94'054'0924   DS102.95

    ISBN 0–434–70315–X

Sections of this book first appeared, somewhat differently, in *Encounter*, *Manna*, *Lillit*, *Index on Censorship*, the *Observer*, *The Sunday Times*, *The Times Literary Supplement*, the *Guardian* and the *Jewish Chronicle*. The author also wishes to acknowledge a grant from the Authors' Foundation, and to thank the library of the Hebrew University for allowing access to the papers of Melech Ravitch.

Photoset by Deltatype, Ellesmere Port
Printed and bound in Great Britain by
Billing & Sons Ltd, Worcester

FOR MY PARENTS,

DAVID AND BETTY,

MY WIFE, FRAN,

AND MY SON,

SETH

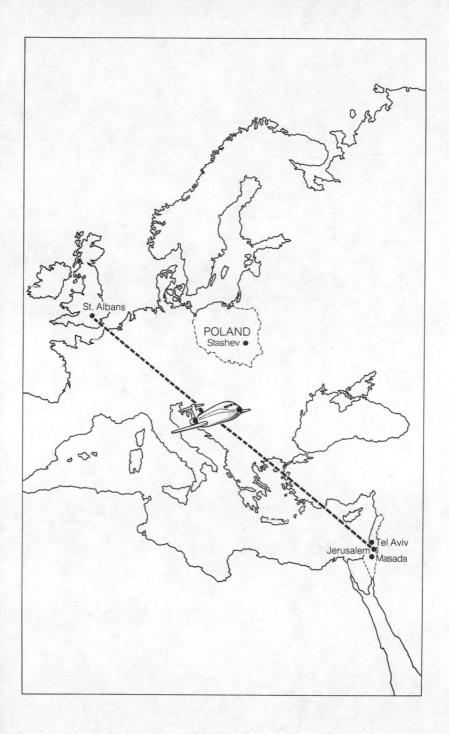

St. Albans

POLAND
Stashev

Tel Aviv
Jerusalem
Masada

PART ONE

THIRTEEN

WAYS OF

LOOKING

AT A

BLACKBIRD

1

BIRDS

'And why,' asks my fellow passenger, 'are you flying to Israel?' 'Research,' I reply, 'I'm writing a book about the place.' 'Fiction or non-fiction?' she asks. 'Non-fiction.' 'Good. Stick to the facts and you can't go wrong.' 'On the contrary, it is easier to tell the truth in fiction.' Finally, the one really memorable line of our conversation. 'My son,' she says, 'has almost dissertated.' I wish that I too, like that lucky boy, had something to prove. But I have no thesis, only a theme. A theme, moreover, I did not know existed until I came to reread the notes I took at the Jerusalem Book Fair in the month of May 1985.

Monday, Jerusalem. My friends have rented the back half of an Arab house on Rehov Harakevet. The front is a synagogue. A wooden sign informs the traveller that it is the Gateway to Heaven. I expect to stay about five nights. Pamela works in the Chinese department of the Hebrew University. Jonathan, formerly editor of an English-language magazine called *Lillit*, now produces films. Yoeli, their second son, wants me to help him make a bird-trap in the garden to catch a pet. We dig a hole, drop in some crumbs, and cover it with netting. No birds fall for it. Later, however, Yoeli finds an injured blackbird. It dies after a few days. A kind heart is not enough, even in heaven's backyard.

3

Tuesday, Jerusalem. Jonathan flies to London. My friend, Josanne, comes up from Herzlia Pituach. I knew her when she had sparrows in her garden. Now she has hoopoes. Not to mention sunbirds in the hibiscus. These are the people I grew up with. How else am I to know that I am in another country?

Josanne loves me for my mind so we go to see the Book Fair at the Binyanei Ha'ooma Convention Centre. Among the hundreds, thousands, of volumes on display I am reminded of the words of another friend, an Englishman, the poet Craig Raine. 'Caxtons are mechanical birds with many wings and some are treasured for their markings – they cause the eyes to melt or the body to shriek without pain. I have never seen one fly, but sometimes they perch on the hand.' I also think of the Hitchcock movie and want to leave. Outside we are stopped by a grey-haired falconer. 'Last night I was on television,' he says. 'Now everyone knows me. You must have heard about my memoirs. I was the famous Jewish spy in the Nazi camp. In America I am selling 3,000 copies every week. My publishers have never known anything like it.'

Later, Ein Kerem. A bird-spotting expedition. Real ones, not books. We park at the end of a dusty track and walk a few metres into a stand of pine. A needle gets into Josanne's foot and she sits down to remove it. Below us is a grove of olive trees, wherein a couple of turtle doves coo. High above, a hungry raptor, probably a lesser kestrel, hovers. Within days a girl is raped on these same slopes and her body burned. Whether the murderer was caught I do not know.

We return to the car and discover that the keys are missing. Locked in the boot, we deduce. A resident, passing with his Alsatian, offers assistance. It turns out that we were both in California at the same time – he in Berkeley doing political

4

science and journalism, while I was down the coast at Santa Cruz studying literature. Now he is a correspondent for 'Cable News' in the States. His house, formerly a shell, is thick-walled and cool. His two-year-old daughter is asleep within. He looks up the names of locksmiths in the Yellow Pages and calls them on his portable Sony telephone. None can come for hours, though one suggests a way of breaking in.

Uri decides to have a go. Leaving Josanne to mind the baby we return to the car. I sit on the boot while he cuts into the rubber seal, pushing the lock this way and that. 'What are your impressions of the mood here?' he asks. I tell him and he tells me how he nearly came to blows with a spokeswoman for Gush Emunim – the right-wing settlers' movement which believes itself to be God's realtor on earth – at a television studio the day before yesterday. The keys are not in the boot but beside the rock where Josanne removed the needle from her foot. Thus was the mystery solved, though not the enigma of the bird in the air.

Wednesday, Jerusalem. Lunch with Yossel and Margaret Birstein at their apartment in Kiryat Hayovel. Yossel is a writer and raconteur. Once, when interviewed, he talked so much that his interviewer first cried then fainted. Yossel tells me the story of a pigeon, told to him by his son-in-law, a zoologist. 'Put a female in the corner of his cage. He makes love. Put a doll in the corner. He makes love. Put wood in the corner. He makes love. Put nothing in the corner. He will make love with nothing till he dies. It's like that with me and Yiddish.'

For years Yossel wrote only in Yiddish. Now he is writing a novel in Hebrew. Based upon the diaries of Melech Ravitch, the Yiddish poet, whose papers he is cataloguing for the Hebrew University. 'I'm beginning to feel like his son,' he says. Thus becoming the brother of our mutual friend, Yosl Bergner, the artist, the legitimate son of Melech Ravitch.

It is the Jewish holiday of Lag b'Omer and in the evening Jerusalem is full of bonfires and barbecues. Shortly before eight Pamela drives me to the Khan Theatre where Milan Kundera will receive the Jerusalem Prize, awarded every two years to the writer who, in the opinion of the judges, best expresses the idea of 'the freedom of the individual in society'.

Kundera is not Jewish, but he has a redemptive image of Israel. It may be observed in a chapter of *The Book of Laughter and Forgetting* entitled 'Angels', wherein he describes how an Israeli student named Sarah responds to her giggly, credulous classmates by kicking the two biggest gulls up the backside. Kundera notes in an autobiographical aside that he too was credulous enough to dance in the magic circle of communism, and that due to the centrifugal force generated by his irreversible departure he is still falling, 'farther, deeper, away from my country and into the void'. 'Sarah is out there somewhere,' he writes in conclusion, 'I know she is, my Jewish sister Sarah. But where can I find her?' In Israel, presumably.

There are many familiar faces in the audience; the publisher Peter Meyer and the novelist Rosemary Friedman among them, taking notes like me. The salutation is delivered by Père du Bois, a Franciscan friar – 'a Christian come to share the history of the Jewish people' – who also happens to be Head of Philosophy at the Hebrew University. He recalls a banner seen in Czechoslovakia after the Soviet invasion of 1968: 'Prague, Biafra, Israel.' Only Jerusalem remains as an example of hope, he says. Promising independence for Czechs as well as Jews. It is a connection Kundera implicitly endorses when he, in his turn, leans against the lectern. 'It is with profound emotion that I receive today the prize that bears the name of Jerusalem and the mark of that great cosmopolitan Jewish spirit. It is as a novelist that I accept it. . . . And precisely in this time of undeclared and perpetual war, and in this city with its dramatic and cruel destiny, I have determined to speak only of the novel. . . . For if European culture seems to me under threat today, if the threat from within and without hangs over what is most precious about it – its respect for the individual, for his original thought and for his inviolable private life – then, it seems to me, that precious essence of European individualism is held safe as in a treasure chest in the history of the novel, in the wisdom of the novel.'

Afterwards there is a party at the House of Quality where Kundera is surrounded by beautiful Czech-speaking Israelis, any one of whom could be Sarah. And me. Kafka could only dream of such a journey, from Prague to Jerusalem. It was his last chance, he thought, to begin a normal life. I want to know if Kundera, now he is here, still feels that Israel is 'the true heart of Europe', a paradigm for all small nations with a culture to protect. And whether it really matters to our disinterested planet? Hadn't Kundera said only this evening that 'great novels are always a little more intelligent than their authors', and hadn't he also written in *The Book of Laughter and Forgetting*, 'Globally the blackbird's invasion of the human world is beyond a doubt more important than the Spaniards' invasion of South America or the resettlement of Palestine by the Jews. . . . And yet nobody dares to interpret the last two centuries as the history of the blackbird's invasion of the city of man'? I don't really expect an answer. Though it is worth considering the following from *Birds of Israel* by Paula Arnold and Walter Ferguson: 'The blackbird is a resident which only lately has spread from Galilee and the Mount Carmel region, where it is common, to the coastal plain.'

7

Thursday, Tel Aviv. Rehov Harakevet means the Street of the Railway. Every morning, before eight, the train to Tel Aviv goes by the house. This morning I am on it. The train rattles through the wild valley of Rephaim. Kek-kek-kek go Smyrna Kingfishers as the engine scares them from their perches beside the polluted River Sorek. On treetops and in the sky Bonelli's Eagles remain unimpressed. What is it to them that trains come and go?

As soon as I arrive at his studio Yosl informs me that he has piles. After three days of suffering Yosl Bergner's piles are public knowledge. He shows me the creams he has already accumulated. By chance I have in a pocket my own ointment for 'embarrassing itching and painful haemorrhoids'. Yosl tries it at once and declares it the best yet. A man arrives with a package of his special cigarettes. They converse in Yiddish. This man's father, Yosl informs me, was a *felcher*, a field doctor in Russia. It reminds him of when he arrived in Haifa from Australia and found Yossel Birstein waiting for him. There was a man in the town selling thermometers, crying in Yiddish, 'God forbid you should ever have to use them.' 'So these are your new Jews,' says Yosl to Yossel, 'they are no different!'

Yosl's new paintings are inspired by the early German *Bird's Head Haggadah*. He began painting bird-headed Jews in medieval European settings, but soon saw that their naivety and zealotry was timeless. Many of the later pictures have desert backgrounds. 'The Jews are calculators, always calculating,' says Yosl, 'so they never see disaster approaching until it is too late.'

On the largest canvas a group of bird-headed Jews sit at a table – a pose borrowed from a Renaissance master – and look heavenwards whither the object of their adoration, a crucified turkey, is ascending. The idea came from a photograph published in *Ma'ariv*, an evening newspaper. It showed a crowd of turkey farmers protesting outside the Knesset. At their head, nailed to a wooden cross, was a turkey.

'This is almost finished,' says Yosl, pointing to a bird-faced Jew perched upon the spire of a cathedral, 'but I cannot decide what to put in his hand. Perhaps a small bird.' Years ago, when his daughter was still a child, he took her to the zoo and they saw a chimpanzee catch a bird. His hand just darted out without the expression on his face changing. Still deadpan, he pulled off its head and handed it to his mate, eating the torso himself.

Later, Herzlia Pituach. The wife of Ambassador Argov, whose shooting was the pretext for the Lebanon War, is on television. Josanne translates for me. She says that her husband hopes that this is not in fact the case. He is shown alert but helpless and depressed. His wife requests an enquiry into the war.

They say that in the North the vultures are fatter than ever. But in Herzlia Pituach, in Tel Aviv and in Jerusalem the blackbirds sing their intoxicating songs, unless they happen to catch the eye of an artist or an ape.

One of Wallace Stevens's most beautiful poems is called 'Thirteen Ways of Looking at a Blackbird'. Israel presents at least as many possibilities; it is a modern state, a biblical anachronism, a socialist experiment, a colonial outpost, a democracy, an occupying power, a small country with a narrow coastal strip, the centre of the world, an orange, a machine gun, a gathering ground for migrating birds, a homeland, an oppressor, a holiday destination, the last resort, the Holy Land, Palestine, Israel. Above all Israel is a nation that believes in the power of the word: Abraham's covenant, the Promised Land of Moses, Herzl's *The Jewish State*, the Balfour Declaration, the Proclamation of Independence, and the pledge, renewed each Pesach, 'Next year in Jerusalem.'

9

What follows is my way of looking at Israel. Where possible I have used my own eyes, though I have not hesitated to use the eyes and voices of friends and acquaintances when necessary. It was never my intention to tell the history of Zionism, but I have not tried to avoid it either. Every text – and in my book Israel is a text, that's the trouble – has its pre-text, without which it cannot properly be understood. As this is hardly an academic book of objective analysis, let me translate that into personal terms: a pre-text is to a book as a hero is to a kid, it is an inspiration, a role model. I have chosen two heroes, one obscure, the other famous, through whom to describe the appeal of Zionism in the long years before I became a sentient being. Both wanted to be other than they were, and were therefore eager Zionists, for Zionism promised to change a whole people. Both are, coincidentally, connected to my friend Yosl Bergner.

2

BUTTERFLIES

The story of our meeting actually begins with another story, which I happened to write in 1970. 'Uncle Vlad' concerns a family of vampires. Although it was included in *The Year's Best Horror Stories* it was really meant to be a comment upon the old campaign between art and life, Uncle Vlad being Nabokov as much as the Impaler. Hence the fearlessly aesthetic feast my sanguinary gourmets prepare for their annual congregation which ends with Crêpes aux Papillons. Three years later, during a short stay in Israel, Josanne showed me a book of Yosl's paintings done between 1963 and 1968 within which was a picture entitled 'The Butterfly Eaters'. When the time came to choose a jacket illustration for my first collection of stories there was, as a result, no competition.

I obtained Yosl's address from the Cultural Attaché at the Israeli Embassy in London and visited him for the first time on Christmas Eve 1978. He lives with his wife Audrey, no less an artist, on Bilu Street, in the centre of Tel Aviv. Nonetheless, Bilu – an acronym derived from *Bet Yaakov lekhu ve-nelkhah*, 'O house of Jacob, come ye and let us go,' and used by some of the early pioneers – is a narrow lane with low, homely buildings on either side, shaded in season by broad-leafed trees. The trunk outside Yosl's house is marked, as if by sympathetic magic, with knots that resemble the philippina-shaped eyes in some of his more surrealistic paintings.

Yosl himself is a one-man Mutt and Jeff. First he snaps something like, 'No, that's impossible,' or, 'I'm too tired today,' but then remorse begins to torment his generous spirit and he ends up giving you far more than you ever suggested. Thus he began our first encounter by making complications. 'The picture you want has already been used on a book,' he said, '*The Instrument* by my late friend Yoram Matmor.' Then, regarding the cumbersome device I had borrowed for the purpose of photographing the original, he remarked, 'You wasted your time bringing that.'

Yosl's studio resembles a memory. In the centre is a large available space filled with anticipatory objects like easels and white canvases, but all around are shelves laden with toys, books, boxes, folders, photos, paintings and ornaments, each of which has its own history. Yosl himself was born in Vienna in

1920, moved to Warsaw in infancy, to Australia just before the war, and to Israel in 1950. It is possible to experience the early history of Zionism by rummaging through these items and waiting for the stories Yosl attaches to them. On his desk that December morning was a recent copy of *Time*, left open at an article on Isaac Bashevis Singer. So I mentioned that I was writing a book about him and his brother Israel Joshua. 'Since he won the Nobel Prize everyone wants to know about him,' he replied, 'but they all get it wrong. Look, *Time Magazine* publishes his so-called Polish passport. Tell me, where are their famous fact-checkers? They should have checked with me. I'd have told them that this is no passport but his PEN membership card. How do I know? Because my father signed it. See, here is his signature.' Suddenly the purpose of my call was forgotten as Yosl recalled the life of his father, the famous Yiddish poet and peripatetic Jew, who wrote and travelled under the name of Melech Ravitch.

Tucked away in Bashevis Singer's memoirs is a portrait which presents him as a Tolstoyan type. 'Ravitch believed with absolute faith that the world of justice could come today or tomorrow. All men would become brothers and, sooner or later, vegetarians too. There would be no Jews, no Gentiles, only a single united mankind whose goal would be equality and progress. Literature, Ravitch felt, could help hasten this joyous epoch.' Melech Ravitch plays no further part in Singer's autobiography as published, yet he remained Singer's friend for all his life. More than a friend, a mentor.

When Melech Ravitch died in 1976 Yosl, anxious to preserve his father's papers, presented them to the Hebrew University. Cataloguing them is no small job, as Yossel Birstein has found, since the papers weigh three tons. To reach the archive – as I did on a subsequent visit – it is necessary to find your way through the windowless corridors of the weirdly empty library on the old Givat Ram campus, until you reach an equally windowless room full of numbered boxes. According to Yosl it resembles an old-fashioned shoe shop. Yossel thinks he looks like the porter in Kafka's story, waiting for what never will come. When told about Yosl's description he cries, 'Marvellous. I'll use it.' 'I already am,' I reply. Either way, the finality of those closed lives presses so heavily on the claustrophobia I am already experiencing that I long to be outside with the living. Yet Yossel is so full of vitality, like a little god, that Melech Ravitch and his circle slowly begin to revive and I wonder if I am not receiving a privileged glimpse of the afterlife.

Melech Ravitch, who knew everyone, threw nothing away. His archive is, consequently, an intimate history of Yiddish culture from about 1920 to 1976, detailing the loves, aspirations, tragedies and complaints of its major figures. No less a gossip than Melech Ravitch's correspondents, I would love to reveal who did what to whom and whose wife did and whose wife didn't, but I am sworn to secrecy. I cannot reveal, therefore, whether it was experience or wishful thinking that led Ravitch and Bashevis Singer to co-operate on a play whose working title was *The Man With Three Wives*. There are notes on scraps of paper throughout the manuscript, as well as sketches indicating the actual staging, which has yet to occur. Since Ravitch left Warsaw for good in 1932, the play must have been written in 1931 at the latest.

'They wanted a money maker,' says Yossel, 'a hit. And how do you do it? By putting in a lot of hot stuff. Free love was a great fantasy for these boys from hasidic or backwoods communities, and the drama was supposed to play out these fantasies – a lot of sex, night after night, here and there.' He shows me a letter sent by a poetess to Ravitch, though it could easily have gone to

Singer. 'I'm waiting for you to come to give a lecture,' she wrote. 'When you come – you know our town is surrounded by woods – we shall walk in the woods and we shall really feel happy about it.' Then Yossel reads me a second letter from the same poetess. 'Oh how beautiful it was in the woods,' she wrote. 'It was the real time of my life. I loved it. I shall never forget it.' Subsequently, she turned up in Warsaw with some poems which Ravitch published. Next Yossel picks out another letter, dated some two years later. 'Melech Ravitch, where did you get lost? But let me tell you what happened to me. I slept with a man for the first time in my life and it was very good.' 'So,' says Yossel, 'the woods were no woods after all.'

After 1932 the situation of the Jews in Poland became less and less like a boulevard comedy. Having left Warsaw, Ravitch became a wanderer. Wherever there were Jews he went. He even went to Sumatra to collect money from the Arabian Jews living there for Yiddish schools in Poland and complained when they didn't give him enough. 'Jews had no foreign offices,' says Yossel, 'so when they wanted to leave a country they wrote to Melech Ravitch, because he answered, and because he had declared that he had torn out from his heart the green envy, the yellow hatred and something else – some red stuff. When other Jews heard about a man with no hatred or envy, a helper, they wrote to him until he became a kind of conscience, the conscience of Yiddish literature. And what do you do to a conscience? You torture it. And this is what they began doing with Melech Ravitch. Even Bashevis.'

When the war was over, Melech Ravitch became a clearing house for the remnants of the Yiddish-speaking communities. A correspondent says he must leave Poland because the earth burns under his feet. 'But tell me please,' he asks, 'Australia, is it very hot there?' Another writer, not yet out of the German

14

camps, says, 'Melech Ravitch, take your pen in your hand and write down the extermination morally and physically of the Jewish nation. But first please send me a coat, not a torn coat, because I am a gentleman.' Ravitch sent a beautiful coat. 'It's not laughable, it's true,' says Yossel, 'the sort of things that were in the minds of those people. They talk, in their letters, as if they were struck by a kind of virus, a mad virus. They're all mad. Their longing is not confronted by any kind of reality. A man in South America thinks, "Oh, New York. Bashevis and I. J. Singer and Leivick and Opatoshu. They must sit there every day and night and talk literature. But with whom have I got to talk in a God-forsaken place like Venezuela?" Now the only two writers who weren't caught by this madness were Bashevis and Joshua Singer (who died too soon). Bashevis looked straight in the eye of the problem and he said, "Let's do something! Masada died a heroic death, let's also die a heroic death." How? Not by taking a revolver and shooting, because he's not much of a fighter. No, he says, "Let's write the great books in the world – you, Melech Ravitch, you write the great poems, I'll write the great books. Let's write the great stuff and die!"'

'I can see that you are a good listener,' said Yosl that Christmas Eve. 'Now tell me again what it is that you want. Butterflies? I have painted a number of pictures on similar themes. Perhaps I can find something suitable for you.' He went out through a white door at the back of the studio and returned, a few minutes later, with a large silk-screen print of 'The Butterfly Eaters'. 'Will this do?' he asked. I nodded. 'Take it,' he said, 'and put that contraption away.'

3

HERO

My butterflies got eaten in the name of art; not so Yosl's. They are the dreams that excited but could not sustain the idealist pioneers after whom his street is named. Not to mention their descendants. The family in Yosl's painting sit around a table in the open air amid sea-green vegetation, some dressed for life in Palestine, others for business in Warsaw. The bird at the foot of the table is half real, half spice-box. Yosl's Jews are literally only half there. They have cutlery and crockery, but no food save blue lepidoptera.

Just as my story was a tribute to Nabokov, whom I took the liberty of addressing as uncle, so Yosl's painting is haunted by the spirit of his Uncle Monyeh. Moishe-Monyeh Bergner, whose photograph dominates one of the walls in Yosl's Proustian studio. It was taken in Palestine in 1911, a few months after his arrival from Poland, by which time the diaspora Jew had shed his disguise, or so he thought, and become his real self, Monyeh Harari (Harari being the Hebrew translation of Bergner, both meaning mountain). In the full-length study the new Monyeh is young and handsome and dressed in the robes of a shomer, the romanticised watchmen who guarded the first settlements, but he remains scholarly and a little melancholy and so looks rather too self-consciously heroic, what with his rifle across his shoulders like a prototype James Dean.

Yosl has produced at least one major painting based upon this likeness, a canvas called 'Hero'. Needless to say, this

16

appellation is ironic, for Yosl's hero has no face. His individuality resides in his costume, which is not as indigenous as its wearer thinks. 'The abbaya resembles a prayer shawl,' explains Yosl. 'The shoes are from Galicia. The pioneers are actors taking part in a play, and someone has changed the scenery behind them without their noticing. The audience, watching, sees the new scenery, but not one of them dares tell the actors that they are acting in the wrong play. From my uncle's letters to his sweetheart I learn that he knew what was happening – but he went on acting, dreaming.' The same figure is central in a group portrait called 'Idealists'. There they sit, these faceless fanatics, unaware that a bird of prey is swooping upon them. Likewise in 'Dreamer' a man reclines upon a barren hillside, blinded by a lepidopterous reverie to the fact that he is at the mercy of ravenous predators.

Recently Yosl gave me a few of his uncle's letters, addressed to his beloved in Galicia, whence came his shoes. The first, sent from Ben-Shemen, an agricultural settlement in the plain near Lod, is full of obvious pride in his manly deeds: 'I have worked here for two weeks. For a long time I worked a ten-hour day at the threshing machines. Yesterday I had a slight fever: of the six who came with me, I was the last to come down with one.' Encouraged by the evidence of his own healthy entrails he makes the following observations and prognostications: 'One comes across wandering Jews constantly here. It seems that there is a tradition of wandering amongst the Palestinians. But there are two kinds of wandering. Here there is a sense of the new, free Jew. Everything is still on the move. It is like an architect collecting granite, basalt, marble and alabaster for a building to be erected according to his orders. Perhaps not much has been built yet in Palestine, but a lot is being done. And one must love the beauty of creation in order to be happy.'

17

By 5 August 1911, however, he is already conceding a little to disillusion. 'A labourer's life knows much beauty, and freedom, not recognising Saturdays. . . . But at the same time, the miserable instincts of a mob hatch unabashedly through the soul's outer crusts. For the soul of a local labourer is not filtered through blotting paper. I would guess that the majority of the workers here were driven, not by their love for Palestine, but rather by the struggle for their daily bread.' He describes his own work and confesses that 'many a weary sigh has risen up to the burning sun of the Palestinian sky', but then recollects that the real purpose of the letter is to persuade his correspondent to join him, and so begins a seductive paragraph that commences bucolically and climaxes cosmically.

'Nature here is splendid: quickset hedges of cactus line the gardens, which blossom with white and pink tobacco flowers, the fruit of the almond trees, and the heavy bunches of grapes hanging from the abundant vines. Along the dusty roads one passes by long caravans of camels, led by the wild Bedouin, and stretching their ornamented heads on long, thin necks. The camels look like wooden statues of indolent white and grey, while the purple, solitary sun sinks somewhere in the distant sky. The clouds cast long shadows on the magnificently carpeted fields, while the mountain peaks are bathed in pink mirages. And beyond these are the stars, whole oceans of sky spread with dark blue sails of the starry boats. And my soul searches in the infinite distances with longing for you, madam. For somewhere in the starry sphere our stars seek too their orbits. . . .' Then he becomes practical. 'With a little courage you could get here soon. I am sure you can find a job as a cook, which is well enough paid. . . . That would be here in Ben-Shemen where the workers' kitchen is very small.'

By 1912, however, Monyeh was in Safed: 'Through the

strong window-frame of a large, third-floor room, from where one looks out upon the deepening blue mountains of Upper Galilee and Jabel Jermaki, valleys overspread with olive trees, and the western sun setting in a blood-burst of crimson – I write this letter.

'But why am I in Safed? You must be curious. I have found that the toil of the spirit and that of the body are of two different worlds. Indeed, I have never intended to remain at work. I assumed that at the end of two years of work, both spiritual and physical (I deluded myself that one can, while working, study, read . . .), I would be able to cast off the yoke of labour. Experience taught me that one has to make a choice between becoming a labourer, a life-long slave to labour, spiritually lost, remaining for ever at the same point (here in Palestine, that of working for the Nation), or becoming a free human being, albeit at the price of parental admonition. I wrote home saying that I no longer want to work, and asked for a monthly allowance of fifty francs: this is quite sufficient for the needs of an idler.

'Since this must come as a shock, I shall enlighten you. Being disinclined to work (I am a loafer to the bone, since work and I are inimical), I had the idea, once sacred, of becoming a shomer. At the time I had just been released from hospital where I lay ravaged by fever. By a lucky coincidence I met the shomrim, and was attracted to them as to the exciting world of knightly heroes, whose eventful lives stem from the hardships of being constantly on guard. . . .'

Accordingly Monyeh became a shomer at a settlement called Nescha. However, during the course of one of his *aduzes* or checks a horse was stolen from under his nose and Monyeh was told, 'Tomorrow you can look for another job.' His description of the incident is confused, full of childish self-justifications

19

and tinged with instability and paranoia. Notice how his attitude towards the shomrim, his fellow watchmen, suddenly alters.

'All this was eating me up. I was no longer talking. Tired, weary and ill, I nevertheless kept up the guard, feeling, in fact, greater empathy for the thieves than for the shomrim, who are, after all, good policemen rather than heroes. There are some heroes too, like my boss, who later grew to hate me so much. On the other hand, there is no shortage of toothless caricatures.'

Monyeh went to Medzel, a farm owned by a society of Russian philanthropists, where he worked throughout the winter, 'lying in the mud, without sheets, wearing Arab shoes, constantly cold and feverish'. Then . . . 'Spring arrived. Wild weeds, red poppies, flowers of the hollies glittering of polished violet, thorny white herbs of the previous year, a whole gamut of colours blanketing the mountains: the same mountains which are overgrown with rocks and stones. Eagles soared through the sky, mightily spreading their black-and-white wings; frogs croaked at night in the reed-strewn wadis. Because of the poor wages, I worked contractually, sometimes earning four francs a day.

'Summer came, with its bistering sun. I revelled in the heat. I worked in forest schools. . . . Acknowledged as a good labourer, I was given better jobs. On Shavuot, while on a walk in the Lower Galilee, I was approached by a member of the Hashomer Organisation to rejoin the shomrim.

'At that stage I was already, in the Arab style, wearing the abbaya and agal. I was able to exchange a few words in Arabic. Strong and healthy, I nevertheless turned down the offer, since my letter asking for money was already on its way home . . . the money arrived. Monyeh packed his belongings on to an Arab mule, and set off for Safed to be idle, go for solitary walks across the mountains, read, smoke the nargila in the way of the Arabs. Live . . . I could see the sand-spread approaches of Judea, the plains of Lower Galilee covered in white stone, the low, tomb-lined, cone-shaped mountains behind Zichron, the beech trees of Mount Tabor, black rocks growing out of the mountains, Arab villages and settlements along the fast-flowing Jordan, the Genezeret Lake, quiet and calm, with blood-red stripes at noon, awesome candles of mountains, praying in the silence of deep waters, palms stretching up to the sky, the white stones of Tiberias, precipices of Wadi Chamam, the Valley of Death, the cliff-hung castle of the traitor Flavius, the tomb of Majer the miracle-maker; wild Arabic dances, beautiful Arab women, and the ominous eyes of the Bedouin: the horsemen's lances and their superb steeds, rocks with fissures and caves, torn apart by the rapid-running stream. I heard how the wild wind howls in the ears of a lonely wanderer, and how melancholy is the sound of the Arab pipe, how the Mediterranean rumbles threateningly at night, and how ominous is the peal of bells mourning the triple-edged sword of cholera. I held in my arms a dying man in hospital, and laughed when he was bothered by the sun. Out of the rocks I hacked graves. I felt the life of Palestine pulsating through me. People here are small. And yet they are deep. There are heroes. There are ageing writers working the land, and sharp-eyed settlers on horseback, who pass by the Arab Sheik riding his silver-spurred stallion, and wearing an abaje and purple dress, armed with a curved white sabre and rifle. I was always alone, and on sleepless nights, with pipe smoke veiling my thoughts, I would watch the lamps with their white, fiery fissures moving around in their crystal-enclosed chambers. I felt alone and, even more, born to be alone.

'I shall remain in Safed for two months. In the meantime I

shall visit all the settlements in Upper Galilee, Jabel Jermaki and the Hermon, twenty-four hours away from Safed. Now that I have stopped working, I feel content. At the first opportunity I shall have my photograph taken, and send you one. I did not receive your photo. . . . You must send me another. I ask this of you urgently.'

'Try to leave as soon as possible,' writes the man born to be alone, 'you will be happy here.'

'Reflected in the glass at twilight, I see my eyes burning with love for you. When we are together, you will let your hair loose and, through those fair flames, I shall kiss your eyes, ardently, passionately . . . let it be soon! Life passes by: this explosive life, full of lust and sin, love and envy, burning with torches of triumph. The wind, blowing in from lonely peaks, casts down the weak from their passes into the wild ravines, and ignites the blood in the veins of the strong. My heart burns with wild hyacinth in my chest, panting with longing for you, companion of my loneliness.'

She came, eventually, but not for Monyeh. Melech Ravitch found her, years later, living in Tel Aviv. She barely remembered his brother, the love of her life. Yosl, however, sitting in the studio that never forgets, muses upon the uncle he never really knew. This is the rest of his story.

Monyeh Harari was in Tel Aviv when the First World War began. He enlisted and fought for the British. Afterwards he attended the Bezalel School of Art in Jerusalem and studied painting under Professor Boris Schatz. He continued his studies in Vienna where he mixed with other Jewish intellectuals. Why did he leave Palestine? From Vienna he wrote to Melech Ravitch, 'The ground is crumbling beneath my feet.' In the summer of 1921 he obtained a gun and threatened to use it on himself. His pictures record this deterioration faithfully. See how the vain youth facing the camera fades, dissolves and is resolved as the anguished man turning his head away in the last, fragmented self-portraits. It is the face of a man who has reached the end of his journey – or almost.

'People who don't really want to die shoot themselves in the stomach,' says Yosl. Unfortunately there were no qualified doctors in the hospital to which Monyeh was taken and he died of his self-inflicted wounds a few days later. After the Second World War Melech Ravitch erected a memorial above his brother's grave, with the names of all the family engraved upon it, so that he should never feel alone. Alongside Yosl's name are the words *Medinat Yisroel*, as if to let him know that his nephew, at least, had followed in his footsteps. 'I'm surprised he didn't put my phone number as well,' says Yosl.

Perhaps it was the legend of Uncle Monyeh, heard in whispers throughout a childhood that coincided with the rise of Hitler, which turned Yosl's head. He played with the paintbox his father had rescued from Vienna and probably imagined what magic images were still locked in those bright colours. Maybe he even felt possessed by his uncle's ghost. Did he see the man with the rifle and the bandoleer coming to life in the westerns to which his father and Bashevis Singer took him?

'He was always my hero,' says Yosl, 'I still have his paintbox.'

Look, should it come your way, at his exhibition entitled *Pioneers and Flowers*, which includes not only 'Hero', 'Idealists' and 'Dreamer', but also 'Swamp', 'Fever' and 'Funeral'. Clearly Yosl is infuriated by the insane theatricality of Uncle Monyeh and his contemporaries, but – despite all he knows – there is love and admiration too. It is an ambivalence best defined by the connection Yosl makes between the pioneers and the flowers. 'My flowers are also fanatics. They are flowers that will never be seen to bloom again. Night flowers which live for a day, water-lilies, swamp flowers, flowers with no name, fruit of the painter's imagination, like glass animals in a once-only jungle land. And perhaps all the stories too about the generation of Founders are merely the fruit of our imagination and our longing for romance, poetry, mystery?' This, above all, is Yosl's subject; the madness of efflorescence, the spectacular brevity of butterflies, flowers and Jews. To which may be added the madness of the artist (or writer) who plays with paints (or words) notwithstanding the mockery of oblivion.

4

THE WOMAN IN THE BOX

So here we are, two loonies, on Bilu Street in mid-April sunshine en route to one of our most prolific allies in the struggle against extinction – the Xerox machine – in order to multiply Uncle Monyeh's letters for the purposes of this book. 'That's Goldberg's house,' says Yosl as we pass the all-seeing tree. 'He opened the first porn shop in Tel Aviv, but the hasids burnt it down. So he started a porno movie theatre instead. Now, he tells me, he can only fornicate by torchlight.' We turn the corner on to Rehov Lunz, where Yosl stops before a patch of dry grass upon which stand a couple of large cardboard cartons, shrunken versions of the apartment blocks that surround them. What instinct caused him to pause? Who knows, but within seconds we are both captivated. Inside are old volumes, magazines, pamphlets and scrapbooks printed in Yiddish, Hebrew and English. I flick through a paperback of feeble jokes and a 1926 edition of the American constitution including notes for immigrants and a guide to naturalisation bilingually presented in both Yiddish and English. 'We Jews are never satisfied,' said Yosl, 'no sooner do we arrive here than we want to go somewhere else.' He takes the book from me and it falls open at a section headed 'Art in America'. 'Come on, let's get away,' he says, as if suspecting witchcraft, 'or else these bloody books will take over our lives.' We turn to go and then see, behind us, a small box beside a lamppost. This is filled with exercise books neatly tied with string. The marbled jackets disclose their Russian origins, but the pages within are covered with neat Hebrew handwriting. 'Don't start reading,' advises Yosl, 'or you'll never stop.' An unnecessary warning – I don't understand Hebrew. 'I think I know who these belonged to,' he says. 'She lived round here years ago. Began as a real beauty but ended bitter and half-mad. See how the handwriting deteriorates. They must be clearing out her apartment.' It occurs to me how nice it would be if this were the library of Uncle Monyeh's lost love.

Yosl subsequently confesses that he kept revisiting the boxes until the municipality carted them away, leaving just a scrap of paper as a souvenir upon the pavement. 'You should have reported the find to me,' says Yossel Birstein later, 'I would have sent a van down from the library to rescue them. On the other hand maybe, just like a person, they had reached the end of their useful lives. Perhaps our writings aren't meant to outlive us.' But Yossel is simply trying to make his friend feel better, he can't really believe what he's said. I remember something he told me about a Yiddish Book Fair he once attended. Yiddish writers know that they have no readers except each other, but they live in hope, and insist that their books are printed on best quality *shmutter* paper so that they will be written into eternity.

5

THIN SKINS

After Goldberg the pornographer and the Woman in the Box Yosl takes me to meet his bootmaker. The shop, little more than a large booth, is advertised by a man-size sole with a smiling face painted upon it. The owner, burly and dark, hands over Yosl's shoes, but angrily refuses the shekels he is offered in exchange. 'He's a crazy man,' says Yosl, 'very violent. I once gave him a framed print and now he says he'll kill me before he takes my money. He is obsessed by hatred for his father. They're a very Latin family. He was imprisoned on an island off Argentina during their Civil War because he was a communist. When he finally got to Israel his father laughed at him. Told him he was a brainless failure. Eventually he learned that his father had a young mistress, so he also married a woman much younger than himself. He is a very unhappy man.' Not a contented soul.

'You and me,' says Yosl as the Xerox machine does its work, 'it's like a plot. We throw down the books and run to the shoemaker where I tell you another story. Now here we are, back with my uncle. There's no escape for the likes of us.' The past is another country and its name is Israel. Israel was founded to redress an injustice, and it has democratically conceded the right to each of its Jewish citizens to correct the mistakes of their ancestors. Sometimes, however, it seems that a Jew's capacity for error is infinite, that each generation is trapped by its parents or children, that Israel, in seeking to redeem the past, is actually reliving it. Certainly the state makes the same promise as Yosl's shoemaker, but then the populace find that they must each cut their new soles from their own skins or – and this is inexcusable – from the hides of their neighbours. The luckier ones simply grow thicker skins, of course, and those of us on the outside secretly envy this animal vitality, only reckoning the loss in moments of unease. These latter-day Esaus are not my subject, however; I am more interested in the thin-skinned, still in search of a *modus vivendi* even in the Promised Land, and not best placed to recognise their own qualities. Let me, then, emphasise the humanity of my friends Yosl Bergner and Yossel Birstein.

Yossel turns up at the studio one day with a band-aid on his cheek. 'Cut yourself shaving?' Yosl asks. 'No,' he replies, 'let me tell you what happened. I was asked to take a photo by a couple who handed me their camera. So I focus on them, ask them to move this way and that. "Come closer," I say. Then the man says, "No, you come closer. I am a skin doctor. You'd better come to see me about that spot. It doesn't look so good." I go to see him and he cauterises my pimple. In a few days I can take off the plaster.' 'Yossel is always the optimist,' says Yosl, 'whenever you see him and ask how he is he always says, "Everything's fine." Maybe after half an hour he'll mention – God forbid – that his daughter or someone is getting divorced. Not like me, the world must know my troubles at once!'

In the catalogue that accompanied the *Pioneers and Flowers* exhibition at the Aberbach Fine Art Gallery in New York the writer Shlomo Shvah made the following observation: 'Yosl Bergner's pioneers are like people without a skin. We see what was happening inside them, the pain and suffering, the alienation, the fanaticism, the excitement and the strangeness. He paints many eyes, black wells, far galaxies reflecting the awe of nothingness. They organise themselves around their eyes, each one concerned with himself. As if the painter paints first the eyes and then the people.'

Thin-skinned himself, Yosl has always loved the thin-skinned, witness his passionate response to Kafka. This is another inheritance. Melech Ravitch was among the first to recognise Kafka's genius, and translated 'The Country Doctor' into Yiddish during the writer's lifetime. After his death he wrote, 'His writing is like the peal of evening bells, whose sound lasts long after.' In 1956 Yosl produced a series of illustrations for a book entitled *Drawings for Franz Kafka*, and twenty years later mounted an exhibition at the Galerie Hardy in Paris called *Paintings after Franz Kafka*. Yosl's images therein are real but intangible, the merest touch seemingly sufficient to shake them out of existence. They are like bubbles of oil in water which hold a recognisable shape for a few moments before re-forming. The life of these bubbles is, of course, surrealistic, but the minute examination of them is not. There is a manic energy in the paintings, as there is in Kafka's writing, which reflects the fear that the image will disappear before it is properly captured, which acknowledges also the impossibility of possession except through the imagination. They are, in short, reports from another country, briefly glimpsed. Let us not beat about the bush, this country is the Promised Land, of which there is but one in the real world. Yosl, like his Uncle

Monyeh before him, dared reach out for it; Kafka, however, could only dream. Perhaps this signifies the difference between a painter and a writer; the former is consumed by the desire to see for himself, whereas the latter is more tongue-tied. The eyes speak a universal language, while the tongue itself is trapped, temporarily at least, by its *mamaloshen*, its mother tongue. Surely this is why Kafka made so many efforts to learn Hebrew, to prepare himself for the escape from the diaspora that never materialised.

6

KAFKA

Beth Hatefutsoth, the Museum of the Diaspora, is situated at Ramat Aviv on the campus of Tel Aviv University. It opened in 1978 to serve two functions; these are, in the words of its guiding light, Nahum Goldmann, 'to create a living memorial of the Jewish Dispersion' and 'to deepen the perception of the youth in Israel' towards the 'amazing phenomenon' that was the diaspora. In 1984 one of its travelling exhibitions, *Kafka-Prague*, came to the Festival Hall in London, and a committee of writers was formed to organise some appropriate cultural happenings. At one of these I met Avrom Shomroni, the *shaliach* of Mapam – a left-wing Israeli, in other words – who expressed surprise at the quality of Kafka's Hebrew, as revealed in a letter on display. This turned out to be – according to

Shomroni's translation – a letter to Puah Bentovim, Kafka's last Hebrew teacher. It was not, I soon discovered, the only time she had featured in Kafka's correspondence.

In a letter to Robert Klopstock, posted in Berlin on 25 October 1923, Franz Kafka mentioned that he had not seen Puah Bentovim, whom he called his 'little Palestinian', for almost two weeks. In November he complained that he hadn't seen her for five weeks: 'She has vanished completely, doesn't answer postcards.' And finally, on 19 December, he wrote, also to Klopstock, 'It's very good that you will be seeing Puah; perhaps then I'll have some news of her. I have not been able to reach her for months. How have I offended her?'

Kafka offensive? There is only one person left who can answer that, Puah Bentovim herself, a woman not unknown to biographers of Kafka, who have provided her with a post-retirement renaissance. At the outset of her career, however, Puah was so keen to be rid of her ailing pupil that when she returned to Palestine in 1925 with her intended she deliberately avoided Hugo Bergmann, another mutual friend, despite her bad conscience. And who can blame her? What attraction could a man with no future hold for a woman so full of plans? Many of which, it should be said, came to pass. She married Joseph Menczel, a fellow teacher, and together they put their educational theories into practice in the new Jewish state. Indeed, inspired by Britain's post-war Labour government, Puah was responsible for the establishment of Israel's first comprehensive school. But, as she is well aware, I have not followed the footsteps of greater scholars to her apartment on Mendele Street in a pleasant suburb of Jerusalem to talk about that, nor about her late husband (whose photographs dominate the living room), but about the obscure writer she last saw sixty years ago.

'I'm not quite so well with my health,' she says, 'two total replacements – artificial – of hip and knee. So now I stay much at home.' Where she receives the curious. 'Even Yasha David, the Commissaire of the Manifestation de Siècle de Kafka – Paris – was here. He brought me two photos enlarged of Puah. Look, in case you need them.' She hobbles across the room to fetch her former self. It is easy to see why this robust, round-faced girl with the thick plaits made such an impression on Kafka; the photographs exude well-being. 'At the age of three I could read,' says Puah, 'at five I have been taken into the elementary school. For ten years in the evening – through the streets of Jerusalem – no lights – I went with my father who had been a teacher in the religious schools – from our home along the Street of the Prophets – to a new House of the Blind, the first one in Israel – my grandfather was among the founders – to teach in the evening the blind, to sing to them, read to them out of the Bible. Every year I became more clever, every year I had more to tell them. Sometimes, in the street, they recognised my voice from far.' Her body may be broken with age, but the voice remains strong, as Puah retraces her steps to Prague. This time around Puah offers the opinion (*pace* the note of 19 December 1923), as we sip tea served by a half-baked German spinster who keeps canaries in her room upstairs, that she was Kafka's last muse.

Actually Puah was Kafka's third Hebrew teacher, though the first to speak the living language. Her predecessor, Professor Thieberger, had been relegated by Mr Kafka to a small dark room on the other side of the kitchen, signifying the status of Hebrew in the household and the larger assimilated community. Puah was promoted to the dining room. She had been encouraged to go to Europe in the first place by Hugo Bergmann, who had gone to school with Kafka. Once there,

31

Hugo's mother had taken responsibility for her welfare. Thus it was to Mrs Bergmann that Mrs Kafka went to obtain Puah's services for her son.

It is a fair bet that Puah hadn't read a word of Kafka's when she began teaching him Hebrew in 1922. So all she saw was a frail man in his late thirties who had been too ill to start the lessons, as planned, the previous winter. 'The moment he recovered a little bit I started to come to his home,' Puah remembers. 'And, of course, with his deep eyes – you know the description of Kafka. He was very tall. He would sit hunched over because he didn't want to show how tall he was. So when he was in company he always bent his head a little bit.' He was so shy that only rarely did he venture a compliment as bold as, 'You look so nice today, with your red dress.' 'Just to recognise that I was a woman,' adds Puah. He was also eccentric. 'Sometimes he would sit on the sofa and laugh, you know, and lie down and laugh.' No-nonsense Puah had 'an attitude to psychology' and waited for the inexplicable mirth to vanish without a comment, never suspecting what 'something was in his mind'. Nor does she know to this day. Thus she asserts, on the authority of Professor Hartmut Binder, that she inspired 'Josephine the Singer, or the Mouse Folk'.

Her reasoning is as follows. Shortly after she reached Prague from Palestine in 1921, Puah got a job with a Jewish Youth Movement. At that time, however, very few German-speaking Jews were interested in Judaism. The children, especially, considered themselves regular little Germans; their idea of recreation was to hike in the woods, build camp-fires, and hold sing-songs. Puah tried to persuade them, by example, to make the songs Hebrew at least, but no one listened. When she mentioned this failure to Kafka, during one of their lessons, he 'just couldn't grasp how it was that they didn't want to learn with such a good teacher'.

Knowing this, Professor Binder has expressed the opinion that when Kafka was writing 'Josephine the Singer, or the Mouse Folk' he must 'have had Puah Bentovim in mind'. Perhaps . . . probably . . . but if so the image of the Palestinian girl singing native songs while her careless pupils chatter in German was only the starting point, the seed of reality that grew, in his mind, into a more fabulous object. Puah's misfortune, which was (if we exclude the ironic element) essentially comic, was thereby transformed into a metaphor for the tragi-comic plight of an artist such as Josephine or Kafka himself. Josephine, like the rest of her race, is a singer in name only, her voice being a squeak. She is, in effect, a self-sustained illusion, her role being dependent upon her skills in self-deception and her audience's platonic conception of what a singer ought to be. She is the memory of a memory or, as Kafka put it elsewhere, a memory come alive. Writing this on the brink of personal extinction, his own voice reduced to nothing by tuberculosis of the larynx, Kafka mercilessly revealed, then threw away, the illusions that allowed Josephine and himself to perform.

Of course the fact that Puah, an undoubtedly brilliant girl, didn't understand him at all was evidence to Kafka of her essential health. If she had been able to comprehend, even slightly, what was really on his mind she would have been useless to him, for she would have been as fearful as Kafka. What attracted him to Puah, aside from her linguistic capabilities, was her innocent vitality. 'I recently had a visitor here, a good friend who lives in Palestine,' he wrote from Muritz in 1923. 'The visit was very brief; she stayed barely a day; but her self-confidence, her calm cheerfulness, remained behind with me as a lasting encouragement.'

It is tempting to see in their brief friendship a metaphor for the relationship between the diaspora and Israel; the one sickly, complex, brilliant, trapped and doomed, the other ruddy, uncomplicated, free and full of plans. Certainly in Kafka's day the diaspora Jew was seen – not only by antisemites but also by self-haters and Zionists – as a parasite feeding off the European body politic. A jackal, in short. So Kafka, himself no Narcissus, constructed a satire at the expense of Western Jewry which he called 'Jackals and Arabs', the Jews being transmogrified into the unsavoury four-legged beasts. The Israeli writer Amos Oz – a Zionist who firmly believes that European Jewry will produce no more Kafkas, thereby demonstrating how Kafka has become, simultaneously, the mark of a culture's potential and a symptom of its exhaustion – has also used the jackal as a symbol. But in his story 'Where the Jackals Howl', the eponymous canines represent the wandering id, the night creatures civilisation cannot tame. They possess also that quality in the Arabs Oz's Jews both fear and secretly admire: an unrepressed relationship with the natural world. The logical conclusion of such a scenario would be a bitter irony; Israel, reduced to a ghetto, would produce Kafkas all right, whose only ambition would be to seek a normal life elsewhere.

And this was Kafka's plan: to start a new life in Palestine. Perhaps there he would be srong enough to outwit the brain-lung conspiracy that was killing him in Prague. The difficulties, however, were formidable. 'Prague doesn't let go,' he wrote as early as 1902. 'This old crone has claws.' Nevertheless, he made a desperate effort to learn Hebrew, not the language of the Bible, but that of Ben Yehuda and Jaffa Street, with the help of Puah Bentovim, a Jerusalemite, the vibrant embodiment of his dreamland. 'As to language,' says Puah, 'Kafka was a genius. We were sitting together between 1922 and 1923 about two hours daily – by that time he had no doubt the whole grammar in his brain – he was longing to enrich his knowledge of everyday life. I have been at that time his only opportunity. . . . He asked, I answered, he looked deep into my eyes, wrote a few notes, very peacefully, still burning with a strong will.'

Puah adds that Mrs Kafka would frequently peep into the dining room to ensure that her son was not overtaxing himself. She had reason, for Kafka devoured the language, hoping that a mind newly fluent in Hebrew would be able to transport a body over the unbridgeable gulf between the present and the future. There was no other way he would get to Asia. Unless he half hoped that Puah would suddenly say, 'Come home with me; I have strength enough for both of us.'

But Puah had her own life to lead. In the summer of 1923 she made up her mind to quit the University of Prague, where she was a student. 'I thought: I'm not a genius for mathematics; anyhow teaching was in my heart.' She told Kafka that she was thinking of applying to an education institution in Berlin and was awaiting permission from her parents. Under the impression that Puah was anxiously watching out for the postman, Kafka wrote her the following letter in Hebrew, which eventually found its way to the Royal Festival Hall.

I do not understand at all your worries over the opposition of your parents to your studies. I thought it was already decided that you would stay in Europe (don't laugh*) another year and a half. Is it not decided yet? And is this question to be decided especially now? By the way, it is not possible for you already to have received your parents' letter with the outcome of Hugo's talk with them. Hugo's wife, with whom I spoke today, still has not had a letter from her husband in

* Kafka added 'don't laugh' because he couldn't write 'Europe' in Hebrew.

Jerusalem. But I well understand the panic with which one waits for an important letter which wanders all the time. How many times in my life have I burned with such anxiety? What wonder that a man does not become ashes long before it appears. I am very sad that you too have to suffer thus, dear, poor Puah.

In fact, by the time this letter was delivered, Puah had taken matters into her own hands and was already in Dresden. A certain Dr Frieda Reichman (future wife of Erich Fromm) had promised to help her and, true to her word, telephoned Berlin in her presence. As a result, Puah was asked to look after thirty undernourished Jewish children who would be spending the summer at the resort of Eberswalde. She had a bad conscience about leaving Kafka, having the same attitude towards 'such people as teaching the blind'.

There could hardly be a more explicit statement of the relationship between pupil and teacher. But if Kafka was nothing more than a blind man, why should Puah be so proud of providing him with inspiration? After all she, representing Israel, has flourished, whereas Kafka, representing the diaspora, is no more – except, that is, for a body of work, now resident in Zion. It is with this second, posthumous body that Puah now claims a relationship. Probably Kafka would have preferred it that way; disembodied love, easier for both.

'I think K loved me as a teacher,' Puah has written of the real man, 'but he never touched my hand.' He was tall, attractive to women. So why did he sit on his hands? Because he knew in his heart that Palestine was beyond him? Certainly it lay across a great divide unknown to cartographers. By reaching over the dining room table and bridging the gap between himself and his Hebrew teacher he would therefore be transgressing holy space.

36

From his point of view, touching hands would have been a blasphemous act, akin to the sin of worshipping the Golden Calf. It would have been to reduce the Promised Land to a lump of flesh, albeit a pretty one. Had he embraced her he could have kidded himself that he had simultaneously taken possession of Palestine. Unthinkable! Kafka more than anyone knew the limitations of language, which were, even so, less than the limitations of his flesh.

That summer he actually promised Hugo Bergmann, visiting Prague on behalf of the Jewish National Fund, that he would be in Jerusalem by the autumn. To test his strength, Kafka decided to accompany his sister to Muritz, on the Baltic, meaning to stop off at Eberswalde; but the detour proved too much and he fainted en route. Puah is in no doubt as to his motivation. 'Of course he was too shy to say it, but when he went to Muritz he still had the deep belief that maybe we should come together and study in Berlin. He didn't know how much I wanted for myself. I mean, it's difficult for a man to think of it.'

At the end of August Puah moved to the Viktoria Heim in Berlin, a boarding school for illegitimate girls which also provided cheap lodging for its staff. Kafka turned up there too. 'He was begging like that, you know, with his eyes, just wonderful, if we can go on studying Hebrew.' After he had departed all the other girls wanted to know whether the tall stranger was a suitor. If so, he was about to be abandoned. Puah had no desire to be the companion of a writer, especially one who would make demands upon her far beyond the call of duty. And this, I deduce, was Kafka's offence. Puah was prepared to offer Kafka a glimpse of the Promised Land but, like Moses, that was all he was going to get.

Kafka died on 3 June 1924, a month short of his forty-first birthday, and was buried, as he knew he would be, in the Jewish

37

cemetery at Strašnice on the outskirts of Prague. There he lies, the eternal son, with his parents, beneath a white headstone that resembles the handle of a dagger. And a pair of monuments, one in Vienna, the other in Prague, stand as solid reminders that two Zionists await their redeemer in alien soil. Their dreams were very different: Monyeh Bergner sought an artistic martyrdom through heroic endeavour, believing that if enough women wept over his corpse he would be revived; Franz Kafka, already undergoing the martyrdom of tuberculosis, merely wanted to live and die as a normal, married man. Monyeh, in short, tried to conquer the land with purple prose and romantic gestures, while Kafka slogged away more modestly at the language of the quotidian. Together they would have made a great team – Monyeh's vitality married to Kafka's sense of reality – but separately neither had a chance, the one too flighty, the other too weak. The real builders of Zion would be practical people, like Puah, strong and determined. But even these practical ones must dream, and it is in their dreams that they have need of Monyeh and Kafka. For they, when all is said and done, are the people Israel was created to redeem.

That is why Israel remembers them; in the paintings of Yosl Bergner and the archives of Beth Hatefutsoth, that 'living bridge' between past and the future. It is true that Kafka demanded of his friend Max Brod the oblivion to which Yosl and I condemned the Woman in the Box, and it is possible that Monyeh Bergner would not appreciate his strange afterlife on his nephew's canvases, but surely on reflection both would accept the posthumous citizenship that has been accorded them. For they have found a home in a country that grants equal status to the living and the dead, in a land of four million that contains five times as many ghosts.

7

BETH HATEFUTSOTH

The trajectory of the arc which began its ascent at the Festival Hall leads me finally to Beth Hatefutsoth itself. In a building designed to give heterogeneous visitors a clear-sighted view of their collective past, there can be few more clear-sighted than its first director, Jesaja Weinberg, who had just resigned when I went to see him, like Kafka, on the rebound from Puah. Workmen empty his desk and remove pictures from the walls of his office while we talk.

The underlying principle of the museum's permanent exhibit was reconstruction, he explains. This presented an immediate problem; in terms of time and space, the history of a people is usually shown in chronological sequence. But in the case of the Jews both time and space are variables. So the presentation is thematic rather than chronological, visuals rather than artefacts. 'It is a "warm" as opposed to a "cold" museum,' says Weinberg, meaning that his intention is to engage the emotions of spectators through their intellects. 'It's probably for most of them the first time they get a comprehensive picture of the history of their own people. If you assume that a normal educated person who went through the English school system comes out with a relatively clear notion of what the history of his nation has been – and the same goes for the French and the Germans and the Americans. It's different with a Jew because he goes through the English system and he comes out with a clear notion and a history of the Britishers, not of the Jews. And the same with the French and German Jews. Here it's the first time for most of those who come that they have the whole picture of the history of the Jews. So this is a kind of experience and it's an experience which apparently raises the Jewish blood pressure a little.

'For those born in Israel it's another story. A great part of those born in Israel, mainly youngsters, are not attracted by the diaspora, have a negative relationship with diaspora Jewry, which, I think, has something to do with the accepted stereotypes of Jewish life in the diaspora as being tantamount to one long series of persecutions, blood libels and martyrdoms; an image of the Jew as the passive victim of non-Jewish virility. I think that my generation has contributed very much to it with our Holocaust education; focusing in Jewish education so much on the Holocaust strengthens this stereotype. The Israelis don't want to identify with that kind of image. There was actually an educational trend here, which goes together with putting all this emphasis on defence and fighting and army, to consider what happened between the destruction of the Second Temple or maybe between Masada and the first immigration wave of modern Zionism as an historical lacuna. Now this museum in a way contradicts this. It contradicts it (a) by trying to steer away from emphasis on the Holocaust and by trying not to become another museum of Jewish death, trying to be a museum of Jewish life, and (b) by showing Jewish life as much as possible in a realistic light. The collective memory of a people normally retains best the glorious victories and the terrible defeats. Now, not having a state of our own we didn't have the glorious victories, we didn't have the armies, so we were stuck with our disastrous defeats. I think we try to get away from that. The other thing is that we took a little away the dust of Jewish diaspora history. Because of the way it is taught in schools, on a relatively obsolete level of didactics, it is dust-covered and the kids are emotionally alienated from it. If the didactics don't overcome that alienation they go through school and nothing sticks. They go through school and they don't know what the hell it's all about.'

'And why,' I ask, 'is it so important that they know what it's all about?' Jesaja Weinberg, I soon learn, retains the values of the *haskala*, the Jewish movement towards the light of European culture, even though that light did for the Jews in the end what my Uncle Vlad did to his moths and butterflies.

'Historical Jewishness,' he begins, 'is a product not of the Judean kingdom but of two thousand years of diaspora life as a minority. It's a certain syndrome which was a product of an abnormal history – it had its negative and its positive aspects, for instance this high level of intellectualisation. It's not here. It was one of the declared aims of Zionism to get rid of it. To become normal. We wanted to become normal. Now you cannot at the same time be Jewish in the historical sense, which is the product of abnormal conditions, and become normal. You pay a price for normalcy.' No more Kafkas, perhaps? 'Now, I'm not saying, "I don't want to pay it," or, "I do want to pay it." I pay it. I'm a product of Weimar Germany. My kids grew up in a home where all the walls are plastered with books, but they don't read them. My home was plastered with books which my father collected, and I read 'em, because I grew up under those conditions. And my daughter, although she shares most of my views – she went to a high school which was left-wing and she learned Marxism there, between biology and mathematics she had lessons on Marxism. But basically she grew up between the cows and the chickens et cetera on a kibbutz, and I grew up in the streets of Berlin, where the Nazis and the communists killed each other, and it's a different story. And my father grew up in a hasidic house which broke down the

41

Bashevis Singer way, and he went out and became secular. The real problem is that the special conditions under which we grew up here, they not only take us away from historical Jewishness, they take us in a certain direction – we are living in a country of colonisation, and colonisation means that you have to fight nature and you have to fight redskins. Let's say that you try to compare the dominant spiritual trends of Americans in the East in the 1880s with Americans in Colorado or Santa Fé et cetera – there was very little liberalism in Santa Fé when they shot the Indians and the Indians scalped them, because it was another world – it was a world of colonisation. There is a certain primitivisation, and there is a certain deintellectualisation of a similar kind, if you compare a kid fifteen years old here and a Jewish normal kid, also middle class, in London or New York or Los Angeles. There are changes.'

At this point, in the interests of a dialectic, I feel obliged to interpolate some extracts from an article I wrote for that extinct Israeli magazine called *Lillit* back in 1970, immediately after my first visit to Masada.

'The surprising difference between history and mythology is that whereas history as temporal truth is temporary, mythology as the fiction of history is constant. Since May 1948 Israel has been an historical *fait accompli* or an accomplished fact on a linear time scale, and as such has been the subject of various interpretations, justifications and denouncements, each of which in its turn has had its season, but then grown sere and yellow, for all written history must meet its autumn. And Clio is a fickle bitch. But mythology is a different matter, the mythology of Israel has no end, each new change, each new cycle, is but a variation upon an established coda; Masada has fallen, Masada shall not fall again.'

In 1970 I was, like many, much vexed by the Viet Nam War

42

and did my protesting on the streets of London and San Francisco, but I was no less vexed by the fashion to equate the Viet Cong with the Palestinians and both with the Red Indians – commies being known as Reds, of course. As a result America lost its past – the Old Frontier – and the cavalry were transformed from saving angels into agents of genocide. I sought to save Israel from this equation. My article continued:

'There is no necessary metamorphosis from Jewboy to cowboy. Nor is there anything necessarily gained from suffering. There is no nobility in suffering, it is only the spectator, that is the cult historian, who glories in martyrdom. Geronimo, the last of the Apache warriors, was finally forced to surrender to his foreign conquerers. He said, "Once I moved about like the wind. Now I surrender to you and that is all." Maybe that is not all. Let the existence of Israel be a symbol of hope for the Red Indians. Are not Elazar and Bar Kochba as much traditional figures within the mythology of Israel as is Geronimo within that of the Red Indian nations? After all, the dodo is dead but the phoenix cannot die.' Amen. What Clio has subsequently done to Elazar and Bar Kochba, not to mention my own views, will be seen in the next part. But for now let us return to Jesaja Weinberg, who has by no means finished.

'There are changes. Those changes also affect the religious part, because religion is also subject to those basic historic influences. And that's what has happened, why the religious are the most violent in this country, violent in the sense of physical violence. They go out shooting the kid in Hebron or the kids in the university or whatever. And they believe in God, and they really do believe, and they are idealists, and they are religious and what have you, and they are as Jewish as my foot is. Nothing to do with Jewishness at all. It has something to do with the vessel of religious form that has got new contents (a) that

43

were determined by the reality here, and (b) which were totally distorted because the normal moral inhibitions which a person carries in his superego were superseded by a misinterpreted authority up in the sky, or deep in the books, which gave you dispensation to do what in normal circumstances you would consider to be amoral, and you do it with God in your heart. So people say, "But they're good kids." Of course they're good kids. They're sure they're doing good, but they are murderers. By all normal standards of judgment. I don't care what they believe, I care what they do.'

'Let us assume some sort of normalisation is accomplished,' I say, 'how will that affect us in the diaspora? Won't it leave us with the choice of aliya or assimilation?'

'Assimilation is a word that has two meanings,' he replies, 'because it (a) means a process, you assimilate a culture of somebody else, you change your identity, and (b) it's also the end product of the same process. When a Jew is assimilated totally, then he's no longer a Jew, he's vanished. But the crucial process for Jews outside Israel in the diaspora in the last two hundred years is the process of assimilation. Assimilation is the Jewish *modus vivendi* in our time. But in that process what is called the Jewish genius – if there is such a thing like that – came out at its best; the clash between the Jewish spirit becoming extrovert after having been introvert in the ghetto for so many centuries, the clash between this spirit and the Western environment was probably the most fruitful cultural experience.'

'But it came to a tragic end,' I say. 'Will the Jewish spirit you've described ever have a renaissance here?'

'Now Israel is again another thing,' he says. 'Since you asked for it I'll put in my nickel's worth. I see it here as an historical process. To begin with the only way of Jewish survival is Israel, because outside assimilation is the dominant force, the dominant process, and I have serious doubts whether in the long run there can exist such a thing as secular Judaism, the diaspora. Jews came here mainly from Eastern Europe. They wanted to remain Jewish, but basically Zionism was anti-religious, anti-orthodox. It was a rebellion against traditional Jewish life. It was actually the antithesis to the basic thesis of orthodoxy – you sit on your ass and wait until the Messiah will come and solve your problems. It said, auto-emancipation. We'll solve our own problems. Now when they came here there were various cultural possibilities. There was no more an identity problem in the sense of becoming non-Jewish by assimilation. You are Jewish almost by citizenship. However, Herzl thought that we'll continue here European culture, and when he wrote his famous book *Altneuland* he thought – maybe I'm exaggerating – but essentially he thought that we'll sit in coffee houses, Viennese style, on the Carmel Mountain and discuss Schnitzler's latest drama. You know, he was very enlightened, so he thought an Arab intellectual, a Jew, et cetera will sit together – speaking German naturally – and discuss Schnitzler's drama. Then when the first settlers came here there was a certain romanticism of the meeting with the Orient and of integration in the environment. And when you see the types of pioneers, the Hashomer organisation for instance' – to which Monyeh Harari-Bergner briefly belonged – 'they had moustaches like Arabs, and they dressed like Arabs, and carried guns like Arabs. And at the beginning Jewish folk music tried to absorb Oriental melodies. Now what really happened? What happened was that we developed into an enclave of Western culture, whether we like it or not. Nothing came out of the synthesis with the Orient. There was a total separation from all Arab, Oriental elements; in the economy, in society, in the culture. And I really believe that we are Western and that the representative expressions of Israeli culture are secular and Western. A clever Jew once said that people make their history themselves, but they make it under given historical conditions over which they have very little control. And that's what is actually happening to us, and what brings about certain discrepancies between what we try to achieve and what we have on our hands.'

Every diaspora Jew has three lives from which to choose, enabling him to live in the past, present or the future. Most, naturally, are content with the present. Others aren't. At Beth Hatefutsoth there is a computer specifically programmed to translate such curiosity into words. And so I take my seat before its keyboard and enter the following words: Smolinsky, Jacobovitch, Pshiskhe, Grodno and Stashev.

PART TWO

TO STAND

DESPITE ALL

POSSIBILITIES

TO FALL

1

JOSHUA SMOLINSKY

My mother's father came from Stashev in South-West Poland. How the Jacobovitch family got there no one knows. His name in Hebrew was Joshua, though he was called Shia, its Yiddish diminutive. When he settled in England it was Anglicised and he became Charles. I am named after him, the initial letter sufficing. My grandmother still has his Russian passport (Russia then, as now, being the area's overlord), in which he is described as illiterate, meaning that he spoke only Yiddish.

My father's mother, who came from Grodno, was named Shaindel. In England Shane became plain Jane. My middle name, John, comes from her. Smolinsky was her married name, which my father changed to Sinclair when he joined the army in 1939. Thus my disguise, my *nom de vivre*, Clive J. Sinclair.

Joshua Smolinsky (whom I might have been) lives, but only in my stories, as a down-at-heel private eye on the seamy side of Los Angeles. Joshua ben David, Joshua son of David, by which I am known to God, has not been heard of since I was called to the bima at my barmitzvah more than two decades ago. The last-named ought to be the essential me, but isn't. I am stuck as Clive Sinclair, because my mother tongue is English.

I recalled my grandfather's passport not so long ago when I found that among the Dover Phrase Books beloved by 'seasoned travellers' was one entitled *Say It In Yiddish*. Just as *Say It In Turkish* implies a country, Turkey, in which Turkish is spoken, so *Say It In Yiddish* also predicates a Yiddish-speaking state. It contains phrases that enable the visitor to pass through customs and passport control, order a taxi to the hotel of their choice, and generally to converse with the population. But where was this country? I couldn't find it in the atlas, so I invented one, situating it in the same provinces of Poland that my grandfather once inhabited (I subsequently learned that a delegation had petitioned the dignitaries at Versailles for just such an entity, but that is real history, not my province). I named the country Ashkenazia, likewise the story in which it appears, and though the narrator claims he speaks Yiddish, I naturally wrote the story in English. In effect, my illiteracy is exactly opposite to that of my maternal grandfather. I am fluent in the language of Pharaoh, as it were, but more or less dumb in that spoken by my ancestors, whether in Egypt, Babylon or Poland. As another of my characters puts it, 'There's a version of the Bible in which Moses attempts to extricate himself from God's command by stammering that his tongue is not circumcised. Well, that's exactly how I felt in Israel; I am Jewish, but my tongue is not circumcised.'

I was born at a time when English history had run its course, and now when my contemporaries speak of the Empire and its end I remain unmoved. No, the matter which really interests me is precisely that for which I have no language. My friend Yosl Bergner, being the son of Melech Ravitch, frequently chides me for including a few Yiddish words in my otherwise pristine English. 'What is wrong with the language you speak?' he says.

Do not mistake my point, I love it. But I am a parvenu, just as I am an exile from my past, of which the occasional Yiddish word is a last reminder. My writing is a search for a place in which I may feel at home, where my literacy will not be in question. Since I am interested in neither sentimental atavism nor utopian visions I have not as yet found it, but if I did what else would I have to write about?

In the main this is desk-bound exploration, of course, requiring neither interpreter nor translator; a journey into hitherto unexplored regions, including the self. I have inherited much from my parents and their parents: my hay fever, my baldness, the colour of my eyes, my appetites, my religion; I have learned much from my universities and my friends, as I would have done anywhere. But I have also inherited something unique from this country – its language, English – my favoured mode of transport. Thanks to it Shakespeare, Pope and Dickens are as much part of my cultural heritage as they are of my more native contemporaries.

Culture, however, is one thing, history another. You can inherit a country's language in a way that you can never inherit its history. I could have made my metamorphosis into Clive Sinclair complete by kidding others (if not myself) that I was a Scot whose forefathers sailed to Britain with William the Conqueror, perhaps by answering in the affirmative to the following: 'Dear Clan-person! Did you realise that you have a Sinclair home from home in the heart of Sinclair country in Caithness? Just a few miles from Sinclair's Bay and the ancient ruined Keep of Sinclair and Girnigoe castles, Barrock House nestles in its woods at the heart of the County. . . . This ancient Sinclair dwelling has been divided into a number of units available for lettings. . . . I hope we may serve you in this respect and that you will be interested to see Barrock House develop over the years as a special retreat where you can find refreshment and relaxation in a location steeped in your own

51

family history.' Saying yes to the letter-writer, Sir John Sinclair Bt, would surely have made me more of an actor than social intercourse already demands. This is not to say that many Jews have not become perfect Englishmen, even Christians, only that I could never be so harmoniously acclimatised. I am not comfortable here, which – again – is not to say that I would be more comfortable elsewhere.

Franz Kafka (who else?) found the perfect words to explain this dis-ease. 'I have one peculiarity,' he wrote to Milena, 'which in essence doesn't distinguish me much from my acquaintances, but in degree a great deal. We both know, after all, enough typical examples of Western Jews; I am as far as I know the most typical Western Jew among them. This means, expressed with exaggeration, that not one calm second is granted me, nothing is granted me, everything has to be earned, not only the present and the future, but the past too – something after all which perhaps every human being has inherited, this too must be earned, it is perhaps the hardest work. When the Earth turns to the right – I'm not sure that it does – I would have to turn to the left to make up for the past. But as it is I haven't the least particle of strength for these obligations, I can't carry the world on my shoulders, can barely stand my winter overcoat on them.' He illustrates this with the example of a man who, before each walk, must not only wash but also sew his clothes, make his shoes, manufacture his hat, whittle his walking stick, and so on. Not that he is particularly talented in any of these skills; as a consequence he is soon exposed, 'naked among rags and tatters'.

To put this letter in context it should be added that it was written in the midst of antisemitic agitation, during which time Kafka walked the streets 'wallowing in the Jew-baiting'. 'Isn't it the natural thing to leave the place where one is hated so much?' he asked in another letter to Milena. '(For this, Zionism or national feeling is not needed.) The heroism which consists of staying on in spite of it all is that of cockroaches which also can't be exterminated from the bathroom.' (Even Kafka couldn't anticipate the ferocity of the exterminators.) The situation in Britain is hardly comparable to that, no one would dare call us bedbugs in public, which does not mean that antisemitism is extinct, merely that Jews have access to Savile Row tailors and Jermyn Street bootmakers, so that they may become counterfeit gentlemen. I speak with some authority; my father's father was a cobbler.

However, I do not want to give the impression that writing about Jews comes naturally to me, or confers some sort of moral superiority. God forbid. No, Western Jews, as Kafka knew, must earn their past. Writing about it thus becomes an existential act, a matter of choice also, but one that at least relates to a history my dumbfounded ancestors could understand. I am, like Yosl Bergner, trying to pay for my boots, boots that were made for me a long time ago. This debt, which can never be redeemed, ensures that there will always be friction in my work, as my almost pristine prose rubs against stories that properly belong in another language. Joshua Smolinsky or Joshua ben David could probably write them better. Or perhaps there is something to be gained from having a language but no history, a history but no language; from being an outsider in England, Poland and Israel. But in such moments as I am experiencing now, as I attempt to find words for my alien thoughts, I think how nice it would be to feel at home in this world, to really be Joshua Smolinsky or Joshua ben David.

2

STASHEV

My maternal grandfather died before I was born, so I heard no stories of his birthplace. My grandmother, his wife, thinks that his family owned an orchard there, but no one knows for sure. There are, however, some pictures of pre-war Stashev in *Image Before My Eyes*, subtitled A *Photographic History of Jewish Life in Poland*, the work of a local paramedic, Avrom Yosl Rotenberg, who studied medicine and photography in Warsaw. Rotenberg began taking his photographs a decade or so after my grandfather's departure, but that is no reason not to retrieve my stolen memories with their assistance. It is certainly possible that Yisrolik Szyldewer, the *baldarshn* or preacher, whose portrait originally appeared in the New York *Forverts* Art Section of 20 May 1923, put the fear of God into the young Shia Jacobovitch. It is also pleasing to imagine that dashing Yitskhok Erlich in his flamboyant jacket gave my grandfather a piggy-back to cheder, as he is doing in the book, for Erlich was the *belfer*, or teacher's assistant, whose job it was to bring children to school and keep them in order once they were there.

There is no one left to ask which school Shia Jacobovitch attended, but there is a group photo on page 88 (by an anonymous professional) of the teachers and pupils of the Mizrachi Talmud Torah. It was taken in the 1930s when my own parents had already met or were about to meet, and Shia Jacobovich had been married a decade and a half (30 August 1917, East London Synagogue), establishing the new relationships that were to lead to the creation of an English family.

Even so I look at the picture as if it were one of my old school photographs and – to my astonishment – I do indeed spot a boy who could pass for my younger self, who might conceivably be the imaginary forebear of the equally imaginary Joshua Smolinsky. The resemblance is confirmed by my Bausch & Lomb reading glass and, more objectively, by my history-teaching wife.

He is sitting in the centre of a front row of thirteen, dressed, like all the other boys, in a jacket buttoned to the neck, the uniform being topped off with a round cap. Directly behind him sits a black-bearded teacher, his hands spread upon his lap, so that they seem to touch the shoulders of my delicate *doppelgänger*, making him, alone among his peers, look a little angelic. This impression is somewhat contradicted, however, by what he is holding in his own hands. For he is fingering, somewhat gingerly, a wooden gun, as indeed are all his fellow pupils, if they are not clutching bows and arrows instead. But they are not playing cowboys and Indians. No, the photograph was taken on Lag b'Omer, the spring festival which commemorates Bar Kochba's revolt against the Romans, and the children are pretending to be his warriors. This would be charming if it weren't for the subsequent history of Stashev – more particularly of these youngsters – which inevitably invests their impersonation with tragic significance. This simple celebration of Bar Kochba's suicidal heroics thereby becomes a horrifying prophecy, an indictment of their smug teachers. Didn't they remember what happened to the 24,000 Talmud students that Rabbi Akiva, the greatest sage of his time, handed over to Bar Kochba in AD 135? All dead between Pesach and Lag b'Omer. What use is a sense of the past if you are blind to the present, what use are wooden guns and toy arrows against the Wehrmacht? But this is an unfair flight, only possible because the unthinkable has occurred.

So let us return to that little boy in the front row who could have been me at five years old. I recognise the melancholy eyes, the pointed ears, the downturned mouth and the tilt of the head, all of which convey the impression that he is not at ease, that he does not belong with this group. How many times did he hear, like me, the words, 'Don't worry, it may never happen'?

It seems incredible that there is less than twenty years between that photograph and another I have, taken at my first school's fancy dress party to celebrate the coronation of Queen Elizabeth II. There are eighteen of us in the photo, including Mrs Blake, our teacher. By coincidence I am standing in front of her, so that her hands rest naturally upon my shoulders, giving me a set of wings to match those of my other self. Like him I am also carrying a gun. In fact there are two cowboys and one Indian among the Little Boy Blues and Bo Peeps. I am one of those cowboys at the dawn of a new Elizabethan age, whereas the kid in Stashev probably still thought himself in Poland by accident. Most likely he spoke Yiddish at home, though the gun is something of an anachronism (perhaps he did, like Yosl, play cowboys and Indians after school), but at school the references must have been exclusively Jewish. Not at the Crest.

My heroes weren't Bar Kochba and Judah Maccabee but Roy Rogers, Tex Ritter and the Lone Ranger. My queen was not Esther but Elizabeth.

Nonetheless in 1979 I visited Stashev.

According to information received at Beth Hatefutsoth, Stashev is a town in the Kielce Province of central Poland, whose Jewish settlement commenced at the beginning of the eighteenth century. By the second half of the nineteenth century descendants of these Jews had established tanneries and shoe factories. In 1932, by which time Jews constituted 57.3 per cent of a population of 8,357, there was a pogrom. No one heeded the warning. On the contrary, at the outbreak of war there were still 5,000 Jews in Stashev. 'The Germans entered the town at the end of June 1941. A ghetto was established in June 1942, in which 5,000 Jews from Stashev and 2,000 from its vicinity were concentrated. The Jewish community was liquidated on 8 November 1942, when hundreds of Jews were murdered and the remainder deported to Belzec death camp. During these deportations many Jews fled to the nearby forests and succeeded in hiding there. After the war the Jewish community of Stashev was not reconstituted.'

We drove there along Route 217 from Cracow, past the smoking and sulphurous chimneys of Nova Huta, below which were prematurely sooty fields of tobacco, and on ninety kilometres or so through agricultural country where everyone else still used the horse and cart. We parked in a big square outside a greengrocery with four yellow pears on display. Opposite was the eighteenth century *Barokowy ratusz z kramami*, which meant nothing to us. We wandered the streets looking for something obviously Jewish, but without Polish or Yiddish we were lost. Was that wooden barn a converted synagogue? Who knew? Not us. Finally I had my wife photograph me at the head of Wysoka Street, a typical row of one-storey whitewashed houses, the rich tourist returned home.

Photographers are everywhere in the town, but their windows are now a kaleidoscope of Christianity; blonde girls with Shirley Temple curls, brunettes with Scarlet O'Hara twirls, dressed in white, always white, hearts emanating rays like sunbursts upon their chests, hands clasped in prayer, eyes bright thanks to candlelight, their faith confirmed. Later these girls or their older sisters marry dark, chunky men with Lech Walesa moustaches and a taste for extravagant bow ties. She holds a bunch of daisies while he holds her. Nine months later

57

they are again photographed, now with a baby between them. Thus life continues in Stashev.

My mother's grandfather came to England in 1885 from Pshiskhe, which is near Stashev. Perhaps he met his future son-in-law at a gathering of landslayt from Kielce Province and, impressed, introduced Shia to his favourite daughter. I have two photographs of Israel Zelinski; the first, a portrait by K. Woolf of the East London Electric Light Studio, shows a confident young man, beard neatly trimmed, moustaches waxed and curled at the tips, eyes looking boldly at the camera. He is sporting a floral bow tie, and the ornate sash of a friendly society, all braid and beehive buttons. The sash itself is marked with the letters T^E, a key, and a tassellated medal, also initialled T^E. But by the time the second photograph was taken all trace of the youthful dandy had vanished. There he stands with his second wife in collarless shirt and tatty jacket outside his greengrocery at 213 Oxford Street, E.1 (Isaac Rosenberg and his family lived just down the road at 159). His beard has gone, replaced by deep lines on the cheeks, and the eyes have retreated. A board bearing his name has been modestly tacked over the professionally painted sign of the original owner. Even so, the seventy-year-old fruit still looks more abundant and appetising than that on sale in Stashev today; bunches of bananas are strung across the window, while shiny apples, grapes, pears and tomatoes spill out of their boxes, and cucumbers are piled high in a Sunlight Soap crate.

Behind the couple, in the doorway, struts a cocky individual in a newly acquired flat cap, their lodger, who has the knowing look of a man who sups nightly from the tree of life. It is a curious image, this wretched man, my great-grandfather, in his borrowed garden of earthly delights. At whose request was the photograph taken? If my great-grandfather ordered it why didn't

58

he smarten himself up? Perhaps he had nothing better to wear but was determined to demonstrate that he had his little spot, a small shop with his name upon it. Sometimes I seek the same reassurance from the books I have written. So what have I inherited from this man, other than an insatiable appetite for fruit? Let's put it the other way round: how is it that I have lost both languages he held dearest?

3

CHEDER

I can hardly be blamed for not knowing Yiddish. Anyway, I have surely paid my dues to the *mamaloshen* with my study of Isaac Bashevis and Israel Joshua Singer and the rediscovery of their sister, Esther Kreitman. Hebrew, however, is another matter. For my parents did make an effort to preserve the Hebrew tongue, by sending me at a tender age to the cheder at the orthodox synagogue in Raleigh Close, Hendon.

Now there is an honourable tradition in Jewish writing of vilification in regard to such places; God-forsaken hovels or torture chambers run by psychotic freaks are described in novels and memoirs by authors as various as I. L. Peretz, Israel Joshua Singer and Henry Roth. From Poland to America, wherever there were Jews, these ghastly places thrived. To be sure, Raleigh Close had been sufficiently civilised by the mores of North West London to ensure that we weren't hit by snuff-smelling demons in black gaberdines, in fact we were taught by women, but even so I was not happy there.

To tell the truth, I can remember next to nothing about the eight or so years I spent in the synagogue classroom, such was the boring uniformity of every hour passed in the custody of those self-righteous pedagogues. If I strain my memory I can just about recall small, grey Mrs Freed who insisted upon a *tzitzit* count every Sunday morning, and sharp-eyed Miss Star with the diamond-shaped specs who lipread every illegal whisper. Punishments were designed to humiliate rather than hurt, and so it happened that my cousin or I would while away the best part of the lesson standing in the corner of the classroom beside the waste-paper basket.

If punishment had become slightly more enlightened since the days of Peretz and Singer, teaching certainly hadn't. Our textbook, *Reshis Da'as*, which for some reason I still own, was based upon a Teutonic model, a fact betrayed by the frequent references to German in the tables of comparative pronunciation, not to mention the actual German that sometimes accompanied the English explanations. What did these strange guttural sounds, born of contorted letters, have to do with me? I was English. Everyone I knew spoke English. As far as I was concerned, cheder was an institution of capricious illogicality, a punishment house to which my parents, otherwise well-meaning, seemed compelled by a force outside themselves to send me. So I rebelled and quietly refused to learn.

Perhaps if Mrs Freed, Miss Star *et alii* had tried to entertain as well as educate me, or at least explained what I was doing there, I might have been more compliant. The only explanation I ever got was that I was there because I was Jewish and that Jewish children had been doing no differently since Babylonian times. Entertainment at cheder? I must have been

60

crazy to have had such expectations! Hebrew – this is one thing I learned – is serious stuff, the history of the Jews being no laughing matter. It is a yoke, and the quicker we were ready to bear it the better, a yoke symbolised by the *tzitzit*, the extra vest Mrs Freed expected us to wear in accordance with God's commandment. Thus as soon as we had mastered the aleph-bet we learned by heart the two great prayers of affiliation and submission: the *shema* and the *amidah*. In Hebrew, of course; no unnecessary nonsense for the benefit of us English thinkers as to what they might mean. Nothing about who composed them or when or why. Moreover, there was the unspoken assumption that this was our real education, that the true function of our most energetic and curious years was to repeat without question incomprehensible prayers and blessings like little Jewish budgerigars. The joke is that the whole enterprise was accidentally undermined by my parents, who knew that what really mattered was how well I did at the Crest and, subsequently, St Martin's. They knew that my barmitzvah was an important symbolic act, but that it was the dreaded eleven plus that would determine the course of my life. There was, in short, a rational explanation for school, unlike cheder. By failing to recognise this simple truth, let alone trying to compensate for it, Mrs Freed, Miss Star and the rest made me seriously question the advantages of being Jewish. My some-time friend Paul, who wasn't, seemed to have considerably more fun.

4

THE FRUIT IS RIPE

We are both in the photograph taken at the Crest in 1953, along with Lawrence Kelvin, Arnold Keller, the only boy to have been expelled from my house, when my mother caught us playing in the coal shed, brainy Jane Reback, Gould Pearson, then my best friend, Barbara Austin, still my friend, John Berg, Lionel King, not so bright, Victor, Lesley and Nigel. A few hundred yards from the school, between Brent Street and Bell Lane, where a shopping mall now stands, there used to be a cinema called the Gala, famed for showing such 'continental' classics as *The Fruit is Ripe*. Except, I should add, on Rosh Hashana and Yom Kippur. On those High Holy days the fleapit was transformed into a synagogue for the benefit of those unable to obtain tickets for Raleigh Close.

It was to the Gala I went with my father at the turn of the Jewish year for meditation rather than titillation, though I was old enough to appreciate the artistry that went into conveying the titubation beneath Sophia Loren's blouse on the posters outside. Within we pushed down our velvet seats, scarred (like Boris Karloff in *Frankenstein*) by overexcited teddy boys, opened the prayer books and followed the lead of our rabbi, who looked on the day like a three-dimensional movie star. If only there had been subtitles, maybe I wouldn't have been so bored with the proceedings. But there weren't, and I was, so my mind wandered to the big screen and the adventures it had seen. Hold the action! What we have here, ladies and gentlemen, is a perfect demonstration of the way assimilation works. Not only is the host culture ubiquitous, it also seems more honest, truer. Reverend Hardman and the cantor, all the congregation, even my father, might pretend that we were in a synagogue, but I knew it was really a cinema. Children don't like to be fooled, they prefer the evidence of their own eyes. That's why I couldn't take Mrs Freed seriously when she tried to kid us that we were really in Israel. I didn't want to know. I wanted real life, not false promises. The fact was that I lived in England.

It so happened that there was a large area of waste ground behind the cinema, an excellent playground when unoccupied by the cars of upwardly mobile youths anxious to try out their newly acquired continental knowledge upon the transient au pair population. Perhaps it was prearranged, I do not recall, but when my cousin and I ran around the corner, on temporary release from the service, Paul was waiting for us. Nor do I really remember if what I am going to describe happened once or several times. All I recollect is that Paul and his olive-skinned friends picked up walnut-sized pieces of gravel and began to throw them at us, their war-cry being, 'Down with the Jews!' We took cover and began a counter-attack. It was fun, if slightly more risky than our normal game of cowboys and Indians, this increasingly unfriendly battle between Christians and Jews. For the first time in my life I thought, maybe it's not so bad being Jewish after all.

5

WINGATE FOOTBALL CLUB

The feeling was confirmed when I became a regular at Wingate Football Club, the only all-Jewish team in the league. We lived near enough to the ground to walk to every home match, whatever the weather. Nor did we miss the aways; my father, after all, was Chairman of the Supporters' Association. The club itself was founded immediately after the war by Major Harvey 'Chi' Sadow, a former Chindit, and three others who were anxious to dispel the belief that all Jews were either fat bankers or walking skeletons. They sought, in short, neither hate nor pity but the respect of their fellows. So seriously did they take their hellenic aim of improving the relationship between Jew and non-Jew on the field of sport that they did not have a man sent off nor even concede a penalty for more than two seasons. Unfortunately, victories were as rare, which certainly made our opponents fond of playing us. They weren't so friendly, however, when we won the London League Cup. But part of the fun of going to Wingate was, I fear, the possibility of encountering just such antisemitism. Football was the thing, but the games would have lacked a certain *frisson*, not to mention intensity and intimacy, if we hadn't all been Jews. Thus I was able to experience my Jewish destiny without the bother of acquiring lost languages. I was not even required to believe in Jehovah. I just needed to be Jewish and love football.

Some years ago, when I was starting out as a writer, I published a story entitled 'Wingate Football Club', fiction built upon memory. It begins, 'There are some dilemmas it is better not even to think about. I'll give you a for-instance. Suppose England were to play Israel in the World Cup. Who would I support?' (Incidentally, I once read the story to a Jewish literary society in Willesden. Afterwards one of the audience, whom I did not recognise, arose and said, 'I used to play for Wingate and I could have written that. But I wouldn't have bothered.' Despite him I shall proceed.) I am actually writing this during the course of the 1986 World Cup; England are there, of course, but not Israel – political considerations having made them part of the Oceania group, which otherwise included Australia, New Zealand and Taiwan. However, during the course of their warm-up England played a friendly in Tel Aviv which, by all accounts, they were lucky to win with a penalty three minutes from time. It was the first occasion the two teams had met at international level – a cause of great excitement, 35,000 turned out to watch – and I had, at last, the answer to my question. I wanted the losers to win.

It is a compliment to Britain that I am able to make such a traitorous confession without fear of the ancient accusation of 'dual loyalties' being flung at me. It might be flung but I do not fear the flinging. Besides, I do have a dual loyalty: to the language of England and the history of Israel. I am, literally, an alienated Israeli. Such a statement might not go down so well among certain circles in America these days.

When I first went to live there in September 1969 the talk on the campus I inhabited was either about Viet Nam or about the verbal brawl between Norman Mailer and Gore Vidal. Now it is Gore Vidal versus Norman Podhoretz, the right-wing editor of *Commentary*, whose views are not normally mine. In the issue of *The Nation* dated 22 March 1986, Vidal wrote: 'Significantly, the one Yiddish word that has gained universal acceptance in this country is *chutzpah*. Example: In 1960, Mr and Mrs Podhoretz were in upstate New York where I used to live. I was trying out a play at the Hyde Park Playhouse; the play was set during the Civil War. "Why," asked Poddy, "are you writing a play about, of all things, the Civil War?" I explained to him that my mother's family had fought for the Confederacy and my father's for the Union, and that the Civil War was – and is – to the United States what the Trojan War was to the Greeks, the great single event that continues to give resonance to our Republic. "Well, to me," said Poddy, "the Civil War is as remote and as irrelevant as the War [sic] of the Roses." I realised then that he was not planning to become an "assimilated American" to use the old-fashioned terminology; but rather, his first loyalty would always be to Israel.'

Is the American language really like an exclusive golf club where alien words must petition for membership? And why is it 'significant' that only *chutzpah* has been accorded 'universal acceptance'? Is it because it denotes, better than any home-grown word could, the essential Jewish characteristic? Do the old-fashioned words snigger every time *chutzpah* opens his mouth, inevitably full of gaucheries, just as Vidal has delicately implanted 'sic' after Poddy's historical slip? No wonder Podhoretz's response was immediate and furious: 'Vidal's every word is drenched in hatred of Jews, whom in the best traditions of antisemitic thinking he portrays as all-powerful conspirators manipulating "us" to further their own nefarious purposes.'

Let us suppose that some patrician writer of English prose or a so-called Young Fogey, citing the above, calls me, as Vidal called Podhoretz, a member of the 'Israeli Fifth-column division'. Should I give myself up and go quietly to the pokey? What, after all, have the Wars of the Roses to do with me? Nothing, except as a means of comprehending Shakespeare's

Henry the Sixth. Nor do I want to become an assimilated Englishman if it involves pretending that my forebears fought with Nelson or Wellington or that I have a family seat in Caithness. And this, surely, is the nub. Vidal is offering Podhoretz an impossible choice: if you want to become a real American you must forget your people's history, an option well known to the psalmists of Babylon, but if you do there will always be Vidals to remind you of your *chutzpah*, to sick upon your *faux pas*. Behind this is the assumption that each nation has its unique story, its own genius, which is inherited exclusively through the genes. And how can a Zionist complain about this?

Indeed, a similar controversy took place in Israel shortly after their team was eliminated from the World Cup. Looking for an excuse Shlomo Kirat, one of the players and a supporter of Meir Kahan, the racist rabbi whose Kach party gained one Knesset seat in the 1984 election, pointed the finger at his two Arab teammates. 'I have long felt that Jewish players cannot give of their best for Israel,' he told the daily *Hadashot*, 'if they have Arab players alongside them. The Jewish state should be represented by Jewish players only.' What is the difference between Kirat's position – out there on the racist right wing – and mine, who supported Wingate because it was an all-Jewish team? There is no doubt the passion it generated waned as soon as gentile players were included. Was I, then, a racist too? Never was there a better example of the theory of relativity, the answer being a matter of relationships between time and space. Wingate was okay because it was the post-war creation of a powerless minority, anyway there were ninety-nine other teams for the goyim to join. But of course there can be only one national side, accessible to all passport holders with the necessary talent. So if an Arab wants to represent Israel he should be welcomed, for Israel – as long as it remains a non-theocratic democracy – signifies more than Jewishness; a nation has its story, but it also has a geography, acceptance of either being sufficient to guarantee citizenship. This is the difference between a club and a country, a difference which Vidal seems pleased to obscure. Now, absolved of guilt, I can return to Wingate, though not before giving the last word to an out-and-out antisemite, Karl Lueger, Mayor of Vienna at the turn of the century. When caught cheering for a Jewish football team, playing the hated Hungarians he snapped, 'It's I who decides who's a Jew!'

'Dear Dave' (the letter was addressed to my father), 'does the name Wingate bring back nostalgic memories? Those blue and white shirts, Hall Lane, Saturday afternoons on the touchline or on the pitch. If it does, then you'll be pleased to know that you will be able to relive some of those bygone days at a Reunion to be held on Thursday, 3 April 1986, at the Empire Rooms, Tottenham Court Road, London. Dinner will be served. Whether you were a player, supporter or just a well-wisher, this Reunion is meant for you to recall happy days when we were all much younger.' It was signed 'Sidney Godfrey', the Scribe that was, erstwhile author of the weekly match reports. Handwritten at the end was this postscript: 'Do hope to be honoured with your presence (& your son?).' Dave's son goes.

Sidney Godfrey, looking not a day older, greets everyone outside the ballroom, and hands us all a self-adhesive label with our name upon it. There are 250 of us. 'I remember this place during the war,' says one old-timer, 'full of Yanks.' Now it is full of faces that I recognise, despite the passage of twenty years. 'Good God,' says Bernie Rothstein, 'look who's here. How's your father? Good, good. You remember me, always the busybody. Is it true that you never married?' 'No,' I say, 'I'm married.' 'Of course he is,' adds his wife, a diminutive white-haired lady wrapped in a fur stole, 'with a face like that.' 'Like his father's,' replies her husband, 'the trouble I had making that man smile. I gave you an education, young man. It's thanks to me that you know how to swear. I hear you've put the knowledge to some use.'

I spot my hero, Allan Tapper, beside the bar, sipping orange juice and leafing through a giant scrapbook. Not red-headed, as I recalled, but balding, the face slightly crumpled, the eyes melancholy. But who am I to make assumptions from facial expressions? 'To me his dizzy runs down the wing were a thing of infinite beauty,' I wrote in 'Wingate Football Club', 'right-backs tumbled to the ground when he passed, felled as if by magic. Pursued by these humbled clods he sprinted for the corner flag and unleashed acute crosses that sent their goalkeeper flailing in the air. Our centre-forward leapt and dived fearlessly to meet the winger's passes. . . .' Ray Phillips, the very man, approaches me as if he had trapped the ball and I were the opposing goalie. 'I don't know your name,' he says, 'but the face is very familiar.' 'It should be,' I reply, 'I watched you play every Saturday for a dozen years.' Ivor Zneimer, a more cerebral footballer, says, 'It's Clive Sinclair, isn't it? I've been reading your stories. You really are obsessed with Wingate. It pops up in the oddest places.' His wife wrote to me in September 1985 after a short feature about my book *Blood Libels*, which also has a lot about Wingate – my Wingate – in it, was shown on BBC2. The producer had traced and used an 8mm home movie of Wingate playing in the 1950s, in which Mrs Zneimer thought she recognised her Ivor. The owner of that film, Eddie Goldberg, is here tonight, shooting the event. In which I am, in truth, an extra.

There is no escaping that feeling, even when my presence is

acknowledged by one of the speechifiers. It is a familiar feeling. Felt most keenly on my first visit to Israel in 1967, just after the Six Day War, when I was glad to be there, though not quite privy to the celebrations. Tonight really belongs to the players, just as that victory really belonged to the soldiers. At Wingate, as in Israel, I was certainly an interested party, but I was on the sidelines, always the spectator, always the sidekick, watching the footballers and the soldiers as they moved from glorious deed to glorious deed. Between us there remains a divide I have yet to bridge. And I suddenly realise that my long association with Wingate was but my apprenticeship for an attempt to establish a permanent affiliation with Israel. I am moving, unlike Gore Vidal, from club to country.

Mr Max Marshall is called to the microphone to propose the toast to the President and the State of Israel, which succeeds, as ever, the loyal toast to Her Majesty the Queen. 'Where better to drink to Israel,' says Mr Marshall, 'than at a dinner given in honour of a club itself named after a great soldier who was both pro-Jewish and pro-Zionist? Tonight, as we raise our glasses, let us think not only of the club we all love but also of the many places in Israel called after Orde Wingate.' One of which is near Netanya, my base in 1967.

6

MASADA

If asked what turned me into a Zionist I generally say, as do most of my generation, the Six Day War. In fact, when the war began in June 1967 I had already booked my ticket for Israel. Why? I wanted to see Masada. It was a new ambition, born of a visit to the Masada exhibit at the Royal Festival Hall on 3 December 1966. I was, at the time, a freshman at the University of East Anglia, from where I made a special trip down to London to see the show. The train ride from Thorpe Station, Norwich, to Liverpool Street was tiresome, despite the fact that I was sharing a compartment with a cadre of sea cadets whose recorded conquests to date seemed to consist of each other's sisters though their scars spoke of more sinister hobbies, so I conscientiously but unobtrusively browsed through *The Jewish War* of Flavius Josephus, which contains the only contemporary account of the fall of Masada.

Flavius Josephus – born Joseph ben Mattathias – was himself one of the leaders of the revolt against the Romans that began in AD 66, eventually rising to become Governor of Galilee, a position he did not hold for long. His description of the siege of Jotapata, during which he commanded the beleaguered Jews, and his subsequent desertion to the Romans, is a masterpiece of hypocrisy, disconcertingly modern in tone. And so Flavius Josephus's voice rose above the self-serving cadency of my carriage to reveal its owner as the great-granddaddy of all those other naughty narrators who unconsciously condemn themselves out of their own months. Including, I confess, the narrator of my own story 'The Promised Land', who begins as a shlemiel trying unsuccessfully to consummate his love for Zion, and ends as a Nazi raping an Israeli.

Jotapata, as Flavius describes it, 'is almost entirely perched on a precipice, cut off on three sides by ravines of such extraordinary depth that when people look down into them their sight cannot reach the bottom.' (To Monyeh Bergner, some eighteen hundred years later, it was still 'the cliff-hung castle of the traitor Flavius'.) Vespasian, however, as Flavius well knew, 'was not going to be defeated either by the natural strength of the place or by the daring resistance of the Jews.' The most daring of whom, according to our eye-witness, is none other than Flavius himself.

When Vespasian's troops almost breach Jotapata's battlements, Flavius, 'thinking it disgraceful if he failed to invent some counter-device to save the town', has a brainwave that wins the day. Flavius, we are told, 'amazed' the Romans. So much so that Vespasian decides to starve the defenders into submission rather than take the town by force, whereupon Flavius hits upon another ruse to dampen the spirits of the Romans. He orders his men to soak their cloaks and hang them around the battlements, so that the walls will run with water. 'The result was despondency and consternation in the Roman ranks, when they saw such a quantity of water thrown away in jest by men who were thought to have nothing to drink.' Vespasian, outwitted, resorts to force, and has the last laugh.

When the outcome is no longer in doubt Flavius is equally ingenious on behalf of his own skin, and offers numerous reasons why his immediate departure would serve the common good. To no avail. 'Children, old men, women with infants in arms wept and fell down before him. They all grasped him by the feet and held him fast, imploring him with sobs to remain and share their lot – not through envy of his escape, I think, but in the hope of their own; for they felt perfectly safe so long as he remained.' Flavius admits that his 'determination to desert them was badly shaken by pity for their tears', but he also observes, crafty devil, that if he yielded 'these appeals would be all, but if he refused he would be watched'. So our hero changes his tune and declares that it would be 'a glorious thing to win renown at the cost of one's life, and by some splendid deed to make oneself remembered by future generations'. Here's irony, given Flavius's eternal reputation – the words are Cecil Roth's – as 'the traitor of Jerusalem'.

Nonetheless, Jotapata's last stand is heroic enough, and Flavius may be forgiven much for his description of it. 'The force of the quick-loaders and spear-throwers was such that a single projectile ran through a row of men, and the momentum of the stones hurled by the engine carried away the battlements and knocked off corners of towers. . . . Getting in the line of fire, one of the men standing near Flavius Josephus on the rampart had his head knocked off by a stone, his skull being flung like a pebble from a sling more than 600 yards; and when a pregnant woman on leaving her house at daybreak was struck in the belly, the unborn child was carried away 100 yards; so tremendous was the power of the stone-thrower. . . . Within the town rose the terrible shrieks of the women, echoed from without by the groans of dying men. The whole strip of ground that encircled the battlefield ran with blood, and it was possible to climb up the heap of corpses on the battlements. The din was made more terrifying by the echoes from the mountain around, and on that night nothing was wanting that could horrify ear or eye. Hundreds of those engaged in Jotapata's death struggle fell like heroes. . . .'

The Romans charge up the ramps built by their slaves. It's all up for Jotapata. But stay! Who is that bloody man who swiftly moves among the remnants upon the ramparts? Surely even Flavius, for it is he, cannot cook up a recipe for salvation at this late hour? Oh yes he can. The ingredients are boiling oil and fenugreek. The former is poured over the heads of the advancing soldiers, so that it runs between armour and skin, the latter goes beneath their feet. Thus defeat is turned to victory as the broiled troops fall flat on their faces. But it is merely a reprieve. A traitor, not Flavius, sees to that.

The Romans take the city and butcher its inhabitants. Forty escape and hide out in a cave. Flavius, of course, is among them. To his horror they decide upon mass suicide, in preference to the invitation of the sated Romans to surrender. 'Are you so in love with life, Flavius,' they cry when he expresses a contrary opinion, 'that you can bear to live as a slave? How quickly have you forgotten yourself!' The jibe is well-justified. Joseph ben Mattathias did indeed forget his former self when he changed his name to Flavius Josephus in honour of his captor. But even so the lotus eater remembered enough to write *The Jewish War*, and to 'bewail my country's tragedy'. No, Flavius did not forget Jerusalem. The proof? His right hand retained its cunning. Take his escape from the cave, for instance.

Ever the pragmatist, our unreliable narrator tells us how he gave up the argument against a glorious death and persuaded his comrades to kill each other according to lots, thereby avoiding the sin of suicide. Slish, slash. Gladly each cuts his neighbour's throat, until only two remain. 'Shall we put it down to divine providence or just to luck?' asks one of them who, having hopped out of the cave and embraced the Romans, goes on to describe Masada's last days with a straight face, consequently providing Gore Vidal's patrician ancestors with a new word: *chutzpah*.

The same Flavius who had campaigned so vigorously against suicide in the aftermath of Jotapata – 'It would be absurd to do to ourselves what we are fighting to prevent their doing to us!' – now quotes with full approval the last oration of Elazar, the leader of the Sicarii. 'Come! While our hands are free and can hold a sword. Let them do a noble service! Let us die unenslaved by our enemies, and leave this world as free men in company with our wives and children.' And so 960 men, women and children perished of their own volition, and when the Romans came upon the corpses of their vanquished foes 'they did not exult over them as enemies but admired the nobility of their resolve, and the way in which so many had shown in carrying it out without a tremor an utter contempt of death.'

Irony of ironies. If Flavius hadn't betrayed the trust of his followers and died with them the eloquent death of Elazar and his comrades would have had no recorder and would have been forgotten. Instead, thanks to 'the traitor of Jerusalem', it has become a paradigm much looked to by the modern state of Israel. Yigal Yadin, excavator of Masada, makes its contemporary significance clear in the booklet on sale at the site. 'However important the finds may be to the scientist, in many eyes Masada was and is first and foremost a symbol. It signifies the stand of the few against the many, the weak against the strong, the last fight of those who gave their life for political, religious and spiritual freedom and chose death rather than slavery and submission. That is the universal meaning of Masada.' Its particular meaning also, for Yadin goes on to describe how, since the establishment of the state, the Israel Defence Force has sworn in the new recruits of its Armour Corps at Masada. 'Even if the place has lost something of "the mystery of its ruins", we are convinced that it will continue to serve as the anvil on which the younger generation of Israel forges its awareness of history – an awareness which will from now on be reinforced with knowledge. "Masada shall not fall again" – in these words the poet Y. Lamdan has summed up the heritage which the defenders of Masada have handed down to our generation; the generation of Israel's revival in its own land.'

75

As for myself, I didn't get to Masada until October 1970. My friend Josanne had emigrated to Israel with her parents a few weeks earlier, about the time of my own return from America. So I merely sustained my eastward momentum and followed her. She was staying at an Ulpan, an intensive language institute, in a one-phone town in the middle of the Negev. I hired a car and one night we drove through the quiet starlit desert from Arad to Masada until we came to the end of the road. There was no youth hostel, that was on the Dead Sea side, only a few cabins in the sand and a barking dog to break the silence, nor any illumination until the beam of a torch returned to its source and became a man in pyjamas. We made him understand with the aid of maps and gestures that we wanted to climb Masada at dawn and he offered us one of his huts for the remainder of the night. The room was filthy, there were rusty razor blades on the floor, a stretcher rested against the wall, incongruous curtains hung from the windows only partly covering broken shutters. There was one grubby mattress on a tarnished iron bedstead. The door opened outwards and had no lock.

I watched as Josanne began to lift her dress over her head, then saw that someone else was watching too. A pair of brown eyes was just visible through a horizontal gap in the shutters. Had they been blue I might have written them off as a reflection of myself, a voyeur and his shadow, but they were definitely brown; for once I was on the inside and it was the Israeli who was the outsider. We left the hut and locked ourselves in the car. As the sun began to rise behind the mountains of Moab we hiked up the western ramp, following the route laid by Silva, his legions and their slaves, and came breathless to the summit. The sky was unfurling like a wonderful pavilion, while the ruins of ochre and tan shimmered in anticipation of their diurnal spotlight, and the distant sea hung like a blue lozenge in suspended animation. And then out come the performing memories. They came unbidden from stone and sand: Herod and his dancing virgins, Elazar and his knife-throwing Sicarii, a military tattoo Roman-style, and finally a few clowns, hermits and wild men. The ringmaster being none other than Flavius Josephus. It's all in the mind, of course, but the blueprint was reality. As if to prove the point I find in a hollow a sesterce of Herod Archelaus: obverse, bunch of grapes on a branch with leaves; reverse, tall helmet with cheek pieces and double crest; emblems chosen so as not to offend the religious feelings of his subjects. Had other rulers been as sensitive and the religious less zealous there might be fewer ghosts at Masada today.

Returning to the desert below we crossed the path of a man who resembled a famous English actor. 'Good day,' he said and then, with a charming smile, added that I would be mad ever to leave such a beautiful girl. But she was not mine to possess, any more than was Israel, and I left both, because my language was English and I had ambitions to be a writer. I didn't know then what my subject would be, nor that I would eventually attempt to possess with the written word what I couldn't otherwise, that I was destined to haunt Masada like that pyjama-clad voyeur, forever spying upon the history of the Jews, stuck at the base camp with the diaspora blues.

7

THE SIX DAY WAR

Of course I knew none of this in the Spring of '67 when I booked myself on a flight from Athens to Tel Aviv, intending to follow in the footsteps of Flavius Josephus, Yigal Yadin and Stephen Adler. Stephen, a schoolfriend, had taken off for a year at the Hebrew University at the same time as I went up to Norwich. His letters soon made it clear that he was getting laid in Jerusalem, indeed it seemed that getting laid was an inevitable consequence of being there, which was more than I could claim for Norwich. The age-old promise made every Pesach – 'Next year in Jerusalem' – suddenly become promiscuous.

Masada and sex, that's what my ticket was for, ancient romance and new experiences.

Then came the extraordinary days when it appeared that Masada might indeed fall again. On 23 May I attended a public lecture given at UEA by E. H. Gombrich called 'The Idea of Progress in Art'. 'It was lucid and interesting,' I wrote in my notebook. 'Gombrich is a big man with a pronounced continental accent. Like his fellow exiles – Berlin and Popper – he is against the notion of progress as inevitable and impersonal. I think the following is an accurate paraphrase of his final remarks: "History does not choose art, man chooses it, and it is up to us to exercise our right." His main point was that the art of one age cannot be compared in the abstract with that of another. They can only be compared if their immediate or expressed ends are the same. Means to express this end may progress. But if the end becomes different the idea of progress is annulled.' Then I noted the day's other talking point: 'A crisis has suddenly developed in the Middle East and an Arab-Israeli war looks more than likely. . . . I would like to think that I had the courage to fight, though I doubt it.' The expressed end of the Egyptians, Syrians, Jordanians, Palestinians and others was to drive the Jews into the sea. To them this would be progress both inevitable and – it is to be hoped – impersonal. The Israelis, of course, had other ideas as to what constituted progress. The means, however, were the same, expressed through more and more sophisticated armaments. When these opposed forces met – with their different ends – the idea of progress was indeed annulled.

On the same day, 23 May, Stephen wrote me a letter from Jerusalem. It arrived a week later. 'As you can imagine things are a little bit tense here at the moment. The UN has cleared out of Sinai, Nasser has closed down the Straits of Tiran to Israeli shipping and the American consulate has advised all Americans to leave Israel immediately. Everyone is expecting a war. Half of the Israeli students have been called up and the university is very quiet. In case you don't quite realise how nervous I am let me tell you that the university is no more than a bullet shot from the Jordanian border. Fortunately we are not expecting much trouble from that direction. Egypt and Syria are the big worries. Many of the American students have been told – not only by the consul but also by their parents – to leave. Some have. Most of us are awaiting fresh developments to make up our minds. . . . If there is war I don't honestly know what to do. Common sense, not to mention responsibility to my parents, tells me to go. On the other hand I would feel terrible about leaving when I have so many friends here, who must stay, and when help may be so badly needed. I am scheduled to leave on 5 July and don't really want to go before, though cowardice may well win out. Many people will enlist, perhaps I will; many will simply assist in volunteer civilian work, perhaps that's for me. These thoughts fill my head, but until the actual moment comes heaven knows what I will do. . . .'

A few months earlier, in response to my letter about the Masada exhibition, he had written, 'Glad you were impressed. The real thing is considerably more impressive, but for God's sake don't get too sentimental over the "Masada shall not fall again" bit. In fact they use Masada for training soldiers by running them up and down it.'

Nonetheless, it was a combination of irresistible potency; the ancient tragedy of Masada and the contemporary threat to the people of Israel. I wrote to another friend, echoing Stephen, 'Can you imagine me getting on a plane to Israel to kill or be killed?' Of course there was self-dramatisation in all this, after all I was young and knew how my own father, in his youth, had gone down to the docks to take a boat for Spain to fight for the Republic (though he had, in the end, stopped short of going). But the tension was real enough, as was my decision.

On Sunday 4 June I went to London intending to present myself at Rex House the following morning as a volunteer; not to fight, but to fill a civilian post vacated by a reservist. By the time I turned up, early that Monday, it was clear that something – no one was calling it a war as yet – had started in the Middle East. Rex House was like pandemonium as scores of volunteers mingled with sightseers, well-wishers and newsmen. Eventually, however, I got my interview. A short man with a walrus moustache, a military type, asked me the following questions. Could I drive? Did I have medical experience? Was I prepared to do any work? Did I realise that I might come under fire? To which I answered yes, no, yes, yes. I was accepted and sent off to the compulsory medical. A couple of hours later a doctor took

80

my blood pressure, examined such urine as I could pass, and observed how nervous I was. I said that I was more frightened of doctors than of Arabs. He nodded and declared me fit. That night I visited Stephen's parents to give them what comfort I could. The lead story on the BBC's television news was a report from their Jerusalem correspondent, Michael Elkins, which, the announcer firmly declared, was 'unconfirmed'. We chose to give it credence. 'Less than fifteen hours after fighting began Israel has already won the war,' Elkins said. 'Egypt is no more a fighting factor. . . . It's the most instant victory the modern world has seen.'

Stephen's last letter, dated 13 June, goes like this: 'The news is a lot better now, of course. As for volunteering to help, I think that they need a lot of people on the kibbutzim while all their young men have been called up. I wasn't in Jerusalem during the fighting because I got stuck at a kibbutz near Ashkelon. Trust me to miss all the excitement. However, today they allowed people into the Old City for the first time. When do you think you are coming out here? I am coming home on 5 July, so I hope we don't miss each other en route.'

In the event my services were not required and I travelled to Israel from Greece (which had its own troubles) on my original ticket, arriving for the first time on the night of 17 August 1967. I joined Josanne, Elizabeth and Marion at the Gali Hasharon, a small hotel in Netanya, a coastal resort some twenty miles north of Tel Aviv, and waited for the morning rather as a theatre audience waits for the curtain to rise. I was not disappointed.

Netanya, like the rest of the country, was in a state of euphoria. Not only tourists but also soldiers, recovering from their wounds in the life-giving sea air, filled its hotels. I shared my own room with an infantryman who had had the misfortune to set off a landmine on the road to Jerusalem, and the good fortune to survive intact to tell the tale. At every table in every café there seemed to be a resurrected soldier ready to enrapture my girlfriends or any other passing beauty with their tanked-up reminiscences. Passing prelims – as I had done, despite my concern over Israel's future – seemed juvenile by comparison. Only much later – when I read *The Seventh Day*, subtitled *Soldiers Talk About the Six Day War* – did I appreciate the psychological damage suffered by these initiates, my near contemporaries. But at the time I envied them their glamour, their sense of camaraderie, of shared experience, I was jealous of their self-knowledge. The feeling of having survived an ordeal with honour was everywhere in Israel that summer. When the local cinema showed a documentary about the war the audience burst into spontaneous applause every time Moshe Dayan or Yitzhak Rabin appeared on the screen. Even I purchased a victory medal, cast in gold, bearing on its obverse the two heroes in profile.

In describing my meeting with Jesaja Weinberg at Beth Hatefutsoth I neglected to mention that it took place at the end of June 1984, during the run-up to what many took to be Israel's most crucial election. Jesaja himself was extremely pessimistic, to such an extent that he feared Israel might become 'fascistic' if the result went the wrong way. Like many on the left he now sees 1967 as a tragic failure as much as a miraculous triumph. 'I think that this glorious victory had some irrational side-effects. There were many people who overnight, as if going through a mental shock, changed their whole world view. I remember a theatre artist, a stage director, immediately after the war when I said something critical or sceptical he said to me, "Jesaja, you know what, Messiah has gone through this country and you didn't even feel it." The guy was brought up by a left-wing youth movement. He was a member of a kibbutz. But suddenly he felt some messianism in his heart. And I think we have here some irrational trends to do with pseudo-messianism. My late friend Nahum Goldmann quoted Nietzsche in a similar context. Nietzsche, after the 1870–71 War, a similarly brilliant victory of the Germans over the French which took a little more than six days but was also overwhelming and brought about the unification of Germany, wrote that it is much more difficult for a nation to digest a brilliant victory than a terrible defeat. And there's no question that spiritually we are suffering from terrible indigestion as a result of a great victory.'

One morning, back in those sweet, salad days of '67, a group of us left Netanya at 5 a.m. in the rear of a military lorry for a brief sortie into captured Egyptian territory. These are the notes I took. 'We went as far as El Arish, where one of the fiercest battles of the war was fought. Northern Sinai is littered with burnt-out tanks, abandoned vehicles, and the empty boots and shirts of the fleeing Egyptian army. A few footprints remain in the sand, disappearing over the dunes. Unexploded shells and unknown mines make it too dangerous to follow them. The local houses all fly the white flag, all are shattered or pockmarked by bullets or shrapnel. El Arish is patrolled by a few Israeli soldiers, one of whom, glad to see us, distributed live bullets as souvenirs. We swam from the otherwise deserted beach, dried under fig trees, and returned to the uncomfortable lorry. Retreating we spent a few hours at Gaza City. Trains loaded with captured tanks, its main square dominated by a ruined tank. Peeling posters of the PLO leader Ahmed Shukeri, the bogeyman who generously offered to assist Jews in returning to their native countries even though, in his estimation, 'none will survive'. More ubiquitous and better stuck are new Israeli posters. The Arabs are either in terminal depression or hyperactive capitalists. Some spit at the sight of us, others crowd around asking for money. Who can blame either? The nationalists regard the Israelis – of whom I am one, bona fide, in their eyes – as invaders, the pragmatists call us tourists. We are pleased when we return to Israel proper.'

8

PEACE NOW

It is nineteen years later and I am once again on occupied territory. It is, to be precise, 14 April 1986, and I am on the road between Jerusalem and Hebron in a Volkswagen with Israeli plates. Pamela is driving. My chauffeuse and my hostess – I am staying in her house, as I have done on every visit since 1970, when I attended her wedding on the eve of my trip to Masada – also something of a confidante and a conscience, politically speaking. Hence our attempt to attend a Shalom Acshav (literally Peace Now) meeting at the Park Hotel in Hebron, being held to counter the extremist Tehiya or Renaissance Party's conference at Kiryat Arba, the Jewish settlement that overlooks the old town.

Overseeing Bethlehem, the first town in the territories, are soldiers on rooftops, their guns as vigilant as lightning-rods or the aerials they complement. The pictures they transmit are fearful. Policemen patrol a crossroads ten or so miles deeper into the West Bank. Some drivers are directed to the left, others are waved straight ahead. We're waved on. However, Pamela stops and asks what's happening. The policeman shrugs. One of his colleagues asks for a ride to Hebron, from where he can get the bus to his home in Beer Sheva. He sits in the back and we feel slightly safer, though Pamela is careful not to commit us to either Shalom Acshav or Tehiya.

The road begins a long but straight decline through rocky fields and olive groves until we can see a leisurely loop that curls towards the east. We can also see that the road is blocked. Buses, coaches, taxis, trucks and private cars are all at a standstill. People wander around, trying to make sense of the situation. At the route's perihelion we observe a minyan made up of settlers, soldiers and Peace Nowniks. In biblical times such a confrontation might have been resolved by a descending *deus ex machina*; today, however, that role is taken by a helicopter containing General Ehud Barak. A few old flat-top houses provide the locals with a grandstand view. Last night, in anticipation of this excursion, I went to see a movie based upon David Grossman's best-selling novel *The Smile of the Lamb*. It is set on the West Bank and concerns a conflict between two old friends, a soldier and a doctor, over their different attitudes to the occupation. The latter befriends an eccentric Arab elder who advises his stateless compatriots to wait in silence while the Israelis destroy themselves. The spectators who line the roofs are witnessing a bloodless rehearsal.

A soldier puts his head through our car's open window. 'You must go back,' he says, 'the road has been closed.' 'By whom?' asks Pamela. 'I am not authorised to say,' he replies. We do not argue. In Israel it is now possible in many cases to deduce the political allegiances of an individual by certain signs about their person. Thus our soldier's knitted kipah and medallion-like Star of David, which speak of the religious right, are more offputting to people of our persuasion than his Uzi sub-machine gun, balanced so dexterously. We bid farewell to our passenger and turn around.

Subsequently we learn that the settlers blocked the road with rocks and that soldiers, acting under orders from General Barak, escorted Shulamit Aloni and other leaders of Shalom Acshav across the barricade. As they pushed their way through the cursing, whistling, shoving and spitting crowd they were called traitors and told to go to Germany, among other things. They spoke, said one of their antagonists, 'words of violence and terror'. 'I was never as humiliated as I was today,' added Shulamit Aloni, who had invited me to Hebron, an invitation I was unable to keep, thanks to the patriotic soldier in the skull-cap.

'The time has come to abandon our illusions,' wrote Yehuda Lahav in the daily *Al Hamishmar*. 'Some of us, misled by sweet talk about "love of Israel", had thought that "those nice boys" from the settlers' movement had meant "to take the law into their own hands" solely *vis-à-vis* the Arabs. Some of us had deluded ourselves that there was some truth to the contention that the murder of Emil Grunzweig had been the work of a lone madman. But at the roadblock on the way to the Peace Now meeting in Hebron, these illusions were shattered. Their terrorism is directed at both Jew and Arab alike. As several of the rioting settlers shouted: the Jews we don't like should be killed even before the Arabs. That's murderous terrorism. It begins with curses, spitting, pushing and stone-throwing. Once things come to blows, the bullets won't lag far behind, and Peace Now members will be the targets no less than were the students at the Islamic College in Hebron. In moral terms, of course, there's no difference between murdering a Jew and murdering an Arab. But politically speaking, the settlers' attack on those attending the Peace Now meeting heralds a new era. It proves that Gush Emunim members and their ilk are aiming at a violent solution not only in their strife with the Palestinians (another people), but also in internal political strife. If one puts it all together – their latent violence, their xenophobia, their fanatical messianism – one cannot but realise that their common denominator is fascism. . . . The intractable opposition to the anti-racism bill, the support given the members of the Jewish terrorists' underground and the action taken to release them from prison – together with the plan (mooted at the latest Tehiya Party convention) to deport the Arabs from Western Eretz Israel [i.e. the pre-'67 state] – are all part of the same picture, which can only be entitled fascism. Professor Yuval Ne'eman [the leader of Tehiya and a cabinet member] may differ from Meir Kahane in that he utters his demand to deport the Arabs without foaming at the mouth; but the plan itself is in no wise different from Kahane's plan, and its promulgation proves that Kahane isn't Tehiya's adversary, but rather its rival. If we don't learn our lessons in time, I'm afraid we can expect some very unpleasant surprises in the future. . . .'

Well, we're not quite sure what to expect as we return to the crossroads where we picked up the policeman and take the back road to Hebron. It is a nervous drive. 'I didn't think to pack the gun,' says Pamela. 'Is it in the glove compartment by any chance?' I look. It isn't. 'You know how to use it?' I ask. 'Jonathan showed me how to fire the thing a few times,' she replies, 'but I don't know if I could now. The mere sight of it is supposed to scare terrorists away.' Maybe she's right; I can't even see it and I'm scared. As a precaution we've taped a Shalom Acshav sign to the windscreen. Trouble is, snipers and stone-throwers aren't much interested in the distinction between Peace Now and Tehiya; to such Arabs our number plates identify us as the enemy. But if I am shot the mistake will be corrected posthumously and I will suffer the eternal indignity of being called a British tourist in the press reports; me, the great peacemaker!

In *The Smile of the Lamb* (cinema version) a donkey, tethered to the road, triggers an ambush. We also encounter donkeys. One, overladen, runs into the path of our car, causing us to swerve; another, less lucky, is already an asinine carcass, its flesh turning to dust, its ribcage exposed. The donkey mediates between man and the elements. We merely seek to come between enemies. The omens, then, are not good. The road ends at Halhul, just behind the settlers' barricade. No trace of their presence remains. The road is open. Coming towards us is an army patrol, overshadowed by a helicopter gunship. They are wary, their guns are cocked. They are not comfortable standing still. 'The demonstration is over,' they say, 'go home.' Only later do we discover the truth, which is that it had not yet begun.

We greet the martial silhouettes on Bethlehem's skyline with relief, and begin to think about dinner. We have, in short, crossed the frontier back into civilisation. Over on the further side are rocky hills and blind valleys which resemble that other Frontier, the Wild West. Certainly I felt like a pioneer, fearful that a bunch of hostiles would suddenly appear on a ridge, as they do in countless movies. It seems that I agree with Jesaja Weinberg after all. There is no question who are the Indians on the West Bank. The only question is whether that situation provides a model for Israel proper. It is raised in Victor Schonfeld's film *Courage Along the Divide*, which graphically illustrates the demoralising effect of the occupation upon both Israelis and Palestinians, still divided psychologically if not politically. It made for uncomfortable viewing. I happened to see the film in company with leading members of the Anglo-Jewish community, both orthodox and dissident, so the discomfort was of two sorts: apoplectic and guilty. Either way it was upsetting to see Israeli soldiers beating West Bank kids, whatever the provocation.

As soon as the lights went up the elders of Zion rose as one man hissing 'Distorter!' and 'Anti-Zionist!' The last being the daftest, for Schonfeld's film is obviously a labour of love, love for Labour that was, personified by Simcha Flapan, veteran peacenik, who says, 'I am for a Palestinian state. Precisely because I am a Jew and a Zionist.'

However, this wasn't sufficient for the secretary-general of the Board of Deputies of British Jews, who would anathematise the programme if he could. He seemed unable to comprehend that he was, by defending the morally indefensible, compromising what would otherwise be inalienable – the very existence of Israel. That which he has just seen, he said, is not the Israel he knows. I do not know it either, but I am not blind, and have seen enough evidence to know that it is there. The ethics of little Israel undoubtedly made conditions in the Occupied Territories tolerable, but as these conditions inevitably deteriorate they are corroding the values that sustain them.

A line must be drawn between the two Israels, moral if not political, so that the one may be isolated from the other. Only a few Jews seem prepared to consider what will happen otherwise. One is June Jacobs, chairwoman of the Board's foreign affairs committee. 'We Jews seem to be frightened of something,' she said, 'but the time has come when we Jews who are courageous enough and proud of Israel have to allow non-Jews to see this film. Something tragic is happening to the Israeli people – they are becoming brutalised because they have to protect themselves.' This may be illustrated by a little story, which is not in the film. It happened at the time of the 1982 siege of Beirut. Uri, a tank commander, goes to a Shalom Acshav demonstration against the Sabra and Shatilla massacres. The police shoot tear gas at the people and Uri, forced to flee, holds his hand over his baby's face. The next day Uri is back in the army on the Gaza Strip. Now it's the local Arabs who are demonstrating. The crowd is getting out of control. Uri gives the order, 'Fire the tear gas!' Which is not to say that I think the film without fault.

There is, curiously, in such a polemic, very little sense of detail – everything seems to happen in the wilderness or in anonymous alleyways for unknown reasons. For example, I only know that the roadblock which stopped Shulamit Aloni's transport was at Halhul because I had been there too. I can think of no better words to describe this absence than those a critical friend, Lorna Sage, used in relation to my own stories. I quote, shamelessly, from a letter. 'Only now have I read the stories – which I enjoyed very much (laughed, winced, puked and all appropriate reactions) . . . As for critical judgments, I've known you too long (though perhaps not well) to feel able to produce such things; I approve in theory of what you're at (?over-kill, can't think of the right way to put it) and revel in it in practice, but there's a kind of middle ground missing.' Lorna didn't mean a sense of moderation, of course, and nor do I in respect of Schonfeld's film. No, what I missed was a sense of diurnal realities, what it is like to be a member of the Palestinian minority. I wanted to know more about its structures and less about its manifestations. There was, in fact, a member of that society present, who could have told us, except that this was a night for gestures.

Mubarak Awad, resident of Jerusalem, is the founder of the Palestinian Centre for Non-Violence, one of whose beneficent acts provides Schonfeld's film with its symbolic climax. Awad and a mixed bunch of Israeli and Arab arboriculturalists go to a private field on the West Bank to plant olive trees. What do olive trees represent? Peace, of course. So what do the Israeli soldiers who come and pull out the saplings stand for? But this is too pat, too stage-managed, a pacific variant of Yasser Arafat's UN appearance with gun and olive branch, equally intent upon turning politics into art for the sake of an audience with sympathy for sale. It would be a great end to a story, but not to a real situation, which requires rather more than politicians with olive trees and stainless shovels for a permanent solution.

'Is this situation permanent?' asked Professor Jonathan Frankel in an article published by *The Jewish Quarterly* in 1985. 'Is the process set in motion by the events of 1967 irreversible?' He is not sure. 'Clearly, only a future shrouded in uncertainty can provide the answer. One form of inexorable logic says that close to one and a half million people cannot be permanently deprived of political rights by a parliamentary democracy in the twentieth century and that autonomy, some form of independence, must result eventually. But is it no less logical to argue that fifty or one hundred thousand colonists, backed by a population ever more accustomed to rule over others, will ever voluntarily permit any such liberation? Which will the future historian perceive as the passing episode: the Greater (but less than democratic) Israel which has developed since 1967 or the Little (but fully democratic) Israel presided over by Ben Gurion, Eshkol and Mapai until that year? Will the earlier era be judged to have contained the seeds of its own necessary downfall? Or will the founding fathers be seen to have built a system morally strong enough to generate one day its own rebirth?'

'The situation is not permanent,' says Tommy Lapid, a man

with the presence of an albino bear, who has been the director general of the Israel broadcasting authority and a political commentator for *Ma'ariv*, and is now Secretary of the opposition Liberal Centre Party, 'but it is bad.' He argues that the territories must be returned to Jordan, not because he is a convert to Palestinian nationalism, but because he is a Zionist – same conclusion as Flapan, different reasons. 'A reactionary Zionist,' he explains, 'I want to live with Jews not Arabs.' In fact he lives with his wife Shulamit, herself a novelist, in an apartment in one of Tel Aviv's older streets, built at right angles to the sea to catch its breezes. I am their guest. Also present is a thin, flame-haired woman of Hungarian origins. 'I am the holder of unfashionable views,' she says 'but I believe that Judea and Samaria are ours by right.' 'You can believe what you like,' says Tommy, 'but you have no answer to the fact that if you have your way Israel will either cease to be Jewish or cease to be a democracy.' 'We are still a young state,' she replies, 'perhaps we have a little more democracy than we need.'

After dinner Tommy watches the news, for professional reasons. Recently he had been interviewed on television by one of his former protégés, whom he had subsequently fired. 'Another interview like that,' the present boss of television is reported to have said to the interviewer, 'and I'll sack you too.' 'What makes you think,' Tommy was asked, 'that you can become a politician when you have such a talent for making enemies?' His wife supplies the answer. 'Suddenly Tommy has become a tolerant man,' says Shulamit. 'Before, he was very short-tempered with nudnik callers, now he listens to their every word.' He proves his popularity by stopping a taxi with a wave of his hand. I shake it and wish him luck.

'That's Tommy Lapid,' says the driver, impressed. 'What a guy! He fought the British in '48. Though don't get me wrong.

92

I'm not for him. I'm for Peres. It was the Likud who fucked us up, not him. Are you Jewish? So why don't you live here? I live here but it's all a big mistake. I should be in New York. I love New York. You think you see me, but you are wrong. My body is here but my soul is in New York.' It is the voice of Flavius Josephus.

9

THE FLAVIUS PROCESS

In *Borrowed Time*, a novel by Amnon Jackont, there is a condition which its discoverer calls 'the Flavius process'. It is defined during the course of a conversation between Father Boniface Orsini, of the Order of St Francis, and Shemesh, an out-of-condition Israeli who has come to Teheran to find his missing friend Arik Ben-Dor (aka Bodinger), beautiful son of a founding father. Boniface begins: ' "In psychology a process is called after the first patient who experienced it. I would call this process in which someone decides to reject his people because he believes that the path they are taking leads to destruction, the Flavius process, after Josephus Flavius."

' "You could also call it the Quisling process."

' ". . . Quisling was a traitor. He handed his people over to the Germans, collaborated with them. Flavius did not do anything to swing the battle in favour of the Romans. He acted by himself and for himself. He tried to persuade the inhabitants of besieged Jerusalem to surrender for humanitarian reasons. In order to prevent the slaughter which, he felt, would be their inevitable end."

' "And abandoning them, changing sides, isn't that being a traitor?"

' "Flavius did not change sides. Neither did Bodinger. They both hid when they saw there was no hope. Bodinger here, with me, and Flavius in a cave, with his friends. The friends committed suicide one by one and Flavius, the only one still alive, emerged from the cave to try and build himself a new life. Does that make him a traitor?" '

In the less dramatic context of the quotidian, though that is often dramatic enough in Israel, the Flavius process simply means leaving for New York, where my taxi driver planned to make his fortune selling electrical equipment, England or Germany. Indeed, Amnon Jackont got the idea in the first place by listening to the conscience-stricken monologues of his friends who already had their one-way tickets and comparing them to the 'historical position that Flavius Josephus had taken'. Perhaps this is to overvalue Flavius's moral worth – after all he expressed no qualms about changing sides – but it is surely significant that the erstwhile 'traitor of Jerusalem' can now be considered as a role model.

Jackont, like most Israeli writers, stresses that his book is primarily a piece of fiction and not a hyped-up critique of society. The disclaimer itself neatly echoes Jackont's theme, which is: 'Why do we have to live up to this myth? To what are we committed, the myth or our own lives?' And what better example of this national myth is there than the story of Masada as told by Flavius Josephus and confirmed, nineteen centuries later, by Yigal Yadin? A myth that informed the do-or-die stubbornness of the founding fathers; who knows if they would have succeeded in building a state without it? But as Jackont says, paraphrasing Ahad Ha'am (the philosopher of spiritual Zionism), every nation has a time for visionaries and a time for priests. In the early days Israel needed its visionaries, but now it has need of priests. Not rabbis, adds Jackont, but priests who can mediate between reality and myth. 'I think that Mr Peres is maybe our first priest,' he continues, 'the first of the new Israeli leaders, who understands that life is a play of alternatives, who does not try to live up to a myth or sell a myth to his people in place of real, important things.'

Shulamit Aloni, a politician, makes a similar distinction. 'You have the kind of liberation movement where people have to stick together and to become enthusiastic and to become more nationalistic because they don't yet have the power, so they use symbols of sacrifice, of heroism. But if you use symbols of sacrifice and heroism after gaining sovereignty and after being strong and responsible for others, then something is wrong. Fighting for independence you have to bring symbols – stronger symbols – to draw people together. But once you are strong you have to bring the things which restrain the power, which is the opposite thing. We have it in the Bible. For instance the story of when the Israelites made war with Jericho. One of the people stole something which caused them to lose the whole battle. And then it was said, if one did a crime all are punished in a collective way because it was in a war and in the beginning. Later on, when the country became settled and the Jews or Israelis became strong and the masters of the land, they changed it. A man is doing a crime and all the people will suffer? No! Everyone will be responsible for what he does. So the way you have in a personal life different stages, you have in a nation's life different stages – every culture needs it heroes, but it is a terrible thing when you change them into a political platform. So every time and situation has its values, and the way people behave when they are ten they cannot behave like when they are thirty years old.'

Which is exactly what Amnon Jackont thinks Israel is doing. 'Once the state had been founded it had a certain period of grace measured by years – not days or weeks – let's say thirty years of grace. And during that time – which was actually borrowed time, because you cannot go on being a wunderkind for ever – during that time things should have happened and they didn't. Instead of really building a genuine Israeli life which is possible to live with, we have been stuck with a myth we were bound to believe in. That's how we wasted the borrowed time we had. Now you may say – as someone does in my book – that the whole history of the Jews consists of borrowed time. We lived from one borrowed period to another, but this is not the way a state can live.'

Uri Avnery is one of the founders of the Progressive List for Peace, a political party that won two seats in the 1984 elections. He is also the owner of a magazine called *Haolam Hazeh*, meaning *This World*, which he acquired in 1950. Put the two together and you get an extremely unorthodox weekly. Like his sometime ally the novelist Amos Kenan, Avnery started his career as a right-wing terrorist, fighting both British and Arabs. But he quickly came to the conclusion that accommodation rather than confrontation was required with the latter. This led to the notion of a semitic alliance, the heart of which would be the twin states of Israel and Palestine. Despite his espousal of Palestinian nationalism Avnery remains a Zionist. In pursuit of this dream Avnery made contact with the PLO in early 1975, establishing something like friendship with Said Hammami and Issam Sartawi, two of the PLO's most sophisticated diplomats. Both of whom were subsequently murdered by Abu Nidal's gang. Eventually, during the siege of Beirut, Avnery crossed the lines of both sides and met Arafat himself. Yes, the hand that is writing these pages has shaken the hand that shook Arafat's. All this is chronicled in Avnery's book *My Friend, The Enemy*.

What I asked him about, when we met at his publisher's, was Masada. 'In the underground looking for inspiring examples of heroism,' he replied, 'we were not only looking towards the Irish and the Polish and the Italian wars of independence, we were also looking to our own history for examples of heroism. For us Masada was not suicide, it was heroism – at that time. We were singing songs about Masada, about Bar Kochba, about all these things. Afterwards, later on, when Israel was created I started slowly to view this part of our history in completely different terms, and I realised that the Maccabees were not basically freedom fighters, really they were involved in a civil war against other Jews who were integrating themselves into the contemporary world. The Maccabees were Khomeini types. They killed everybody who didn't agree with them. They killed everybody who was playing football. Because football, or whatever it was at the time, was a Greek institution. Then I started to think about the downfall of the Jewish commonwealth. . . .' The consequence of this rethink was a series of articles in *Haolam Hazeh*, reconsidering the heroics of Elazar and Bar Kochba, among others. Indeed, Avnery claims to be the first latter-day Zionist to denounce Bar Kochba's folly. In place of those suicidal heroes Avnery would like to see Herod ('a remarkable diplomatist, defamed by the religious'), King Saul ('dethroned by a religious fanatic'), and King Solomon. Diplomats and compromisers all. Time to dip swords in ink, rather than blood.

10

THE BAR KOCHBA SYNDROME

It is shabbat in Jerusalem and my hosts, Pamela and Jonathan, have an open home. At present they live in Talpiot on Rehov Klausner, just inside the old border. Among the visitors this afternoon are the Shines and the Silbermans. Sam Shine is a child psychologist. When asked how he is he says, 'Fantastic.' When asked how his day has been he says, 'Excellent.' When asked if he would like a drink he says, 'Great.' Recently there has been a spate of teenage suicides in Jerusalem; for example, a boy from a good family shot himself without explanation and a year later, after his memorial service, his best friend did the same. Whenever these things happen Sam Shine waits anxiously until the victim is named, praying that he or she is not one of his clients. We blame the situation. Perhaps these kids have been infected with a peculiar strain of Kahanism, which allows them one radical solution to otherwise insoluble problems.

Jonathan mentions that his company, Scopus Films, has been approached by Menachem Begin's son. It seems that Benyamin Begin is trying to raise money for a dig at Betar and wants Jonathan to produce a promotional film for showing to sympathetic audiences in the States. Betar is a rocky hill overlooking the railway from Jerusalem to Tel Aviv. At its summit are remains the local Arabs call *Khirbet al-Yahud*, the ruins of the Jews. Betar is the site of Bar Kochba's last stronghold. It is also – and this is no accident – the name of the youth movement of Herut, Menachem Begin's former power base. In the second instance Betar derives from the Hebrew initials for Berit Yoseph Trumpeldor, the League of Yoseph Trumpeldor, called in honour of the latter-day saint of Revisionist Zionism. 'People don't know or don't want to know,' says Shulamit Aloni, 'that the right wing in Israel – Herut, Betar – was based upon Italian fascism. Vladimir Jabotinsky, its founder, saw nationality as more important than human rights. He had the same uniform as Mussolini, the brown shirt, and the same way of thinking: that the person is only important if he serves the big ideal.' If Trumpeldor, killed defending the settlement of Tel Hai in 1919, is Betar's lost leader, Bar Kochba is its glamour boy. In fact the Bar Kochba Syndrome, first described by Yehoshafat Harkabi, one-time director of military intelligence and now Professor of Islamic History at the Hebrew University, is the exact opposite of the Flavius process.

Bar Kochba, you'll recall, was the leader of the second revolt against the Romans which began in AD 132 and ended three years later with the destruction – according to the Roman historian Dio Cassius, writing more than fifty years after the event – of 985 villages, fifty fortresses and 580,000 Jews. Bar Kochba himself died at Betar, and with him went the last trace of Jewish independence for eighteen centuries. It was, wrote Dio Cassius, 'as if the whole world raged'. There was, however, no Flavius to perpetuate Bar Kochba's words. The few contemporary documents that have been recovered refer to him as Simeon Bar Koseva. The name Bar Kochba, meaning Son of the Star, actually came from Rabbi Akiva, who hailed him as Israel's Messiah during the revolt's triumphant overture. Out of the ruins, however, came a third name, a pun on the first: Ben Koziba, from the root *kazav*, meaning false – the false Messiah.

A contemporary equivalent might be Ariel Sharon, the

former Minister of Defence, who masterminded the Lebanese invasion of 1982. This should be borne in mind when reading Professor Harkabi's description of the revolt of AD 132. 'If the failure of the Bar Kochba revolt stemmed from a mistaken assessment of the possibility of defeating the Romans – well, mistaken assessments are frequent to the point of banality in the annals of mankind. The question is not how Bar Kochba and his coevals erred, but why we should treat their error as something to be revered; how is it that a people comes to admire its own destruction. . . . This positive evaluation of the revolt is, moreover, a manifestation of appalling national callousness, disregarding as it does the price of the revolt in loss of life and in the suffering of tens of thousands, perhaps hundreds of thousands of victims . . . as though all this were of no account, a price that we, today, could afford to pay. Is it not faulty thinking to venerate one who inspires heroism without regard for its consequences? Historians will continue to study the Bar Kochba revolt, but the image the public has of a given historical episode has less to do with the real nature of the event than with the mental world of that public. The fact that I have been taken to task for having undermined the Bar Kochba "myth" suggests that there is a cognitive unbalance in this country, reflected in the belief that national disadvantage derives from a lack of daring . . . overlooking the fact that daring can be disastrous. The same holds for national aggressiveness, which instead of bringing benefit can lead to ruin. The blind worship of dare-devilry and a policy of recklessness causes every fantasy to become a kind of vision and fantasists to appear as statesmen. . . . True, it was not the Bar Kochba revolt that engendered this cast of mind, but our attitude to that revolt is symptomatic.' These are not the views of those who want to find sponsorship for the excavation at Betar.

'What should I do?' asks Jonathan, a leftist, but no radical. I am in two minds. There is no doubt that Professor David Ussishkin, the archaeologist in charge of the dig, is motivated by scholarly interests. 'If you ask me what I'd like to find,' he has said, 'I'd like to find writing, but I don't expect to find it.' I find the business of archaeology fascinating, especially when it has such a story attached, witness my response to the Masada exhibition (identified as the 'Masada Syndrome' by Dr Daniel Bar Tal, another diagnostician). But I also accept that times have changed and that the picture of a militant nation state surrounded by enemies and prepared to exercise the Samson option, as peddled by Herut, is no longer appropriate for Israel. There comes to my mind the image of those Polish schoolboys, posing with their Lag b'Omer weapons, and I wonder what my other, lost, self would make of a Bar Kochba cult. It is time to say something on behalf of those pupils who have not yet been led to the guns by misguided teachers. To use Professor Harkabi's distinction, it is the moment for strategists not tacticians, for Peres not Sharon. There is a further complication: Betar is situated on the Jordanian side of the old border, the green line, made redundant by the events of 1967.

'Don't do it,' says Neil Silberman. Neil is an American with the combative personality of a tennis ace, though he actually does most of his work in the archaeology department of the Hebrew University. His special interest is the uncanny relationship between political propaganda and archaeology. There are, it seems, several academics who no longer accept Yadin's interpretation of the finds at Masada. They do not question his integrity, but rather seek to show how, in his anxiety to confirm Flavius and thereby help consummate the link between language and land, he made his discoveries fit the story that pre-existed in his mind. A story, moreover, that owed as much to the prevailing styles as it did to the actual events. According to Neil, Elazar's oration was included to flatter a Roman demand for noble antagonists. Nor did the Jews complain, until now.

'I agree with Neil,' I say, 'don't do it.' Thus Masada falls again, as the myth flies out of the window. Even so, my feelings for Israel, which have no foundation in either religion or language, remain miraculously free-standing. Paul Klee puts it thus: 'To stand despite all possibilities to fall.' That's me, and my Zionism. We stand despite all possibilities to fall. There's a touch of paranoia here, I confess, but there are, nonetheless, plenty of gravity's allies around, ready to shake the stability of the Jewish body politic. As yet, I regret, no one has come up with an antibiotic that will palliate Arab anti-Zionism, which makes it equally hard to cure the Bar Kochba or Masada Syndromes.

11

THE GARDEN OF GETHSEMANE

Back in England I turn on the radio for news of Israel and learn that a British tourist has been shot while knocking at the gate that leads to the Garden of Gethsemane. A real Englishman, a Protestant, who met his assassin where he should have found his saviour. I know the spot well. I too had an encounter there, though the Arab who approached me merely wanted my money. 'You are English?' he asked. I think in English, even when I don't think English. So I confessed that I was. Always. 'I go to London,' he said, 'in winter. It was very cold. Here I used to go with an English lady. Kathleen Kinyon. You know of her? I was an assistant. Now I have a collection of coins. I would sell to the Rockefeller, but I don't want to pay taxes. Last year a boy found a silver shekel in a field. He sold it to the museum for thousands of dollars. I have this for you.' He opened his hand to reveal a small bronze coin; his mouth, also ajar, disclosed a huge build-up of plaque on his teeth. 'It is a denarius of Bar Kochba. You may have it for ten dollars.' I get it for five. Later, at the Israel Museum, I identify the coin as belonging to the reign of Agrippa I, earlier than Bar Kochba, but neither so rare nor so emotionally charged.

Some years separate these two incidents, one tragic, the other comic, but I am convinced there is a connection between them. Let us suppose, for the sake of argument, that the same Arab sold me the dud coin and murdered the pilgrim. What is the common denominator? The answer is Bar Kochba. The Arab first tries to ingratiate himself by selling relics of a Jewish hero then, failing that, emulates his methods, preferring nihilism to pseudo-numismatics. The Bar Kochba Syndrome, in short, is not confined to Israelis. Such is the ironic predicament of the Palestinians who, while hating Israel, draw their inspiration from it. Jewish history, too, with its phases of exodus, diaspora and ghetto, is frequently used as a model for their plight; thus one of the bitterest twists of the Lebanon fiasco was that while Begin compared Arafat to Hitler in his Berlin bunker, Arafat likened his situation to that of the Jews in the Warsaw ghetto surrounded by Nazis. No less galling to all concerned is the fact that the present, despised Jewish state affords a rehabilitatory glimpse of what those who speak of a

103

democratic Palestine must have in mind. This, surely, is one of history's cruellest jokes. Here's another, for those who feel that the world would be a safer – if not a kinder – place without nationalism.

12

THE LAST JEWISH JOKER

Along with his white tuxedo, black tie and spats, Katz the comedian packed a fossilised fish. It was his lucky mascot. And being down on his luck Katz needed that fish. The trouble with him was that he couldn't keep his mouth shut. Once the Hollywood big shots doffed their hats to Katz, now he couldn't even get employment as a jester at a wedding. Katz's last American performance brought the house down – on his head. 'Samson didn't do it better,' said his ex-agent. Called before the committee to name names, Katz had studied the papers they placed before him. 'You think you have given me food for thought.' he said. 'Pish! It's not even fit for cats.' So saying he chewed up the documents and spat the pulp into the faces of his accusers. Afterwards, in Israel, he made a living as a *badchen* at the posh weddings of the pseudo-orthodox. But his jokes became harder and harder to swallow. Guests began to complain that fish hooks were slipped down their throats while they were helpless with laughter. The invitations dried up.

Plotz, an entertainments officer with Zim shipping, owed

Katz a favour. Passengers on the voyage between Marseilles and Haifa needed constant amusement to keep them contented. Plotz thought that Katz, a former Hollywood star, might be a novelty. Katz, a terrible sailor, accepted the assignment. 'Please,' begged Plotz, 'no politics.'

Katz did some research. He read up on flying fish and dolphins, often encountered at sea. Dolphins make wonderful mothers. They lactate upon their sides so that their offspring may receive the full measure of their milk. Their mouths are fixed in beatific smiles. The outward journey was uneventful. Before Katz properly got his sea legs they were in Marseilles. After dinner on the first night of the return Katz showed the audience his lucky mascot. He pointed to the fossil with its sloping forehead, gaping eye sockets, prominent mouth and said, 'Ladies and gentlemen, as you all know by now we are descended from fish. The cadaver you see before you is the great-great-great-great-grandfather of Prime Minister Begin. "Never again!" he screams, inspired by the fate of his ancestor. But he is a chip off the old block, being fixed in his ways. His inheritance is a heart of stone. The remains were found in Lebanon, you'll be relieved to know, which proves that we have been in the Middle East since the beginning. Yes, this proto-Begin flopped from the primeval soup into Lebanon's warm mud with a delightful plop. That was easy. Getting out was another matter. As you see, he never did. Mud sticks.' At which point several outraged passengers began to pelt Katz with their *hors d'oeuvres*. The barrage of *gefilte* fish forced Katz to retreat. 'A lively crowd,' he commented. 'Watch your tongue,' begged Plotz.

Next night you could have cut the atmosphere with a knife. 'Let's talk about dolphins,' said Katz. Everyone relaxed, even Plotz. 'Beautiful swimmers,' he continued, 'as smooth as a

105

Cadillac Eldorado. So what else is new? Their brains. Pound for pound an average dolphin's brain is bigger than Trotsky's. That's big. Some scientists even say the dolphin is the brainiest creature on God's earth – counting the oceans.' He paused. 'Have you seen the size of their *shnozzles*? The rabbis are investigating. If a bunch of *schwartzes* in Ethiopia can be Jews why not dolphins? Here's a true story. At the crack of dawn some rabbis row out to sea mumbling the morning prayers between their grumbles, wondering whether the patriarch of the deep, Leviathan himself, will appear with dripping *tefilin*, when wham-bam they are knocked ten feet in the air by an overprotective mother who mistakes them for fishermen. As the rabbis sink to the bottom Mrs Dolphin says to her little ones, "It's a miracle they didn't catch you and turn you into cat food. Next time, perhaps, you'll listen to your mother." Once settled upon the ocean floor the rabbis question the dolphins on matters of *halakhah*. Do they only eat fish with scales? How is it possible to light shabbat candles underwater? Although the answers are satisfactory the rabbis are suspicious. They pine for Jerusalem. The dolphins urge their *kvetching* guests to abandon nationalism and become rootless cosmopolitans, but eventually agree to transport them to dry land. One morning a dozen dolphins leap out of the Mediterranean near Haifa and toss the hasidic cowboys on to terra firma. "Nu?" ask the people. "Are they Jews?" "No," reply the rabbis, "they are too happy. They have no complaints."' The laughter was spontaneous, no harm in making fun of rabbis. Only Katz looked glum, he had forgotten how to laugh. 'Cheer up,' said Plotz, 'they like you after all!'

As if Katz cared! He looked at his former audience, now feeding itself upon compote and *lokshen* pudding, and envied its appetite. The ocean's swell and the ship's lullaby made him feel queasy, as if the world didn't make him sick enough. Nevertheless, he had a vision. Instead of the greedy contingent presently filling the dining room of the *M.V. Dan* he saw a ragged, unformed bunch of illegal immigrants crammed into the hold of the *Beria*. Katz, who had changed his name from whatever it was (taking the prefix from the eponymous hills), underwent a further sea-change. No longer a broken old cynic thrice disillusioned – Europe, America, and now the home of homes – but a pioneer, who told jokes full of hope and kept up spirits with his *joie de vivre*. Bitterness, his constant companion, was a stranger. Until Plotz tapped him on the shoulder. 'You look tired,' he said. 'Of everything,' replied Katz. He staggered to the deck and saw Cyprus glittering on the horizon. Formerly he would have looked out for Aphrodite, but at last he was past caring. Let her rise from the waves, he knew which direction he would choose.

The steward found Katz in the bath when he arrived to make the bed. Katz looked like a synthetic fossil encased in perspex, but his body slipped easily enough from the liquid matrix. 'Dropped off and drowned,' concluded Plotz.

They dressed Katz in his tux and spats and sewed him up in an old sailcloth, putting the last stitch through his nose to make sure he wasn't playing possum. There were a few prayers and even a tear or two and then the old comedian took his final bow. Katz fell among dolphins who grinned as if he were still cracking jokes. They beat the ocean with their flippers in mock applause until, weighed down, Katz disappeared forever.

13

SHLOMO THE GIRAFFE

First Monyeh Bergner, then those suicidal teenagers, now Katz; it seems that the realities of life in the Middle East extract a high price from romantics, for whom disappointment in self or others can result in a terminal sulk. And me? To whom sulks are not unknown. Am I on the side of the dolphins, as a reader of 'The Last Jewish Joker' may logically conclude? Are rootless cosmopolitanism and the diaspora blues admirable states given the paraphernalia God's bride now needs to protect her integrity? No, no, I think highly of dolphins but consider, on the whole, that they've taken the easy way out, evolutionally speaking; no, to discover my political views you need to read me on giraffes, the living emblem of Paul Klee's dictum; in particular Shlomo the giraffe – narrator of my story 'The Evolution of the Jews' – who made his debut in the letter columns of the *Guardian* about the time of Israel's first Lebanese invasion, the Litani Operation.

Friday, 31 March 1978
Sir – it seems that there are lessons for man in the deaths of giraffes. Poor Victor taught Englishmen how dangerous it can be to be bashful in mating. First comes extinction of self, then of species. Now the death of Shlomo in Tel Aviv zoo has come as a warning to Israel. How did he die? Through over-reaching. He fell while trying to eat leaves from a tree in

a neighbouring enclosure. Let us hope that Shlomo did not die in vain.

The following correspondence ensued:

Wednesday, 5 April 1978
Sir – Clive Sinclair (Letters, 31 March) says that the death of Shlomo the giraffe in Tel Aviv zoo is a warning to Israel not to over-reach itself. In fact, Shlomo died because an artificial fence denied him access to his natural habitat.

Thursday, 13 April 1978
Sir – Surely the trouble with Shlomo the Tel Aviv giraffe was not that he was fenced in, but that he was a foreign immigrant living out of his natural habitat?

I was allowed the last word:

Wednesday, 19 April 1978
Sir – I expected someone to claim that giraffes have no place in Israel. But Mr Bickerdike (Letters, 13 April) is quite wrong. May I refer him to a painting by Bartolommeo di Giovanni hanging in the Fitzwilliam Museum? It is called 'The Story of Joseph', and among all the camels in the caravan of the sons of Jacob there is a single giraffe. And Jacob's giraffe begat . . . unto Shlomo, Israel's latest prophet.

I also received a private letter from Manchester. The writer, mistaking me for an anti-Zionist, issued this challenge: 'Of course you might know of a PLO statement in which they recognise Israel's right to exist within agreed borders as a self-determinedly Jewish state. Equally you may know of some means of guaranteeing Israel from being rocketed and shelled from across her borders by PLO irredentist extremists should two mutually recognisant states of Arab Palestine and Jewish Israel agree on a border. I shall be delighted to be referred to such information by you.' I replied with a précis of the foregoing. He, in turn, was much relieved to discover that my name concealed a Jewish presence, and not 'one of the variety of sanctimonious retired KCMGs and other CAABU types' it suggested. No such problems for Oz, Sobol, Dor, Lapid, Amichai, Yermiya *et alii*.

PART THREE

NO

OLYMPUS

IN

ISRAEL

1

LIONEL DAVIDSON

In a way this book began with that article on the mythology of history I wrote for *Lillit* in 1970. I had gone public – albeit to a small audience – and I liked everything about the experience; from writing through proof-reading to collecting the airmailed magazines from the Israeli Embassy in London. Above all, I liked the research. I spent most of May 1971 staying with Pamela and Jonathan in Jerusalem, working with the latter on the fifth issue of *Lillit*.

I saw *Saint Joan* at the Habimah Theatre in Tel Aviv and wrote my review on a portable typewriter in their back room the following day, coming to the conclusion that the play was really a disguised pantomime; I sat in the shadow of a palm tree in the lemon-scented atrium of the American Colony Hotel photographing Ronald Segal, editor of Penguin's African Library, while Jonathan and others interviewed him, oblivious of the seedy green bird shit that dropped about me; I hung around the editorial office on the campus of the Hebrew University and then drove down with copy to the hot metal shop where I watched the typesetters, who couldn't read English, carefully pick out the correct letters with tweezers until each slug of type was full and locked into a chaise. Also I wrote 'The Story of Daedelus and Icarus' for the magazine and interviewed my first writer.

113

I sent Lionel Davidson a letter on *Lillit* notepaper. 'I'd like to meet you,' he replied, 'but stating a date and a time is difficult. I'm building a house and there always seems to be a plumber or an electrician about with a lot of problems. Why not ring up one morning and see how I'm fixed, and, if feasible, pop down?' I popped. We talked. I informed him that his best books, *The Rose of Tibet* in particular, combined the pukka thrills of Rider Haggard with a semitic mistrust of history and its self-appointed agents. He seemed pleased with that, though we disagreed on what were his best books. 'In turning into an Israeli have you ceased to feel British?' I asked finally. 'No,' he replied, 'I won't cease to be British. For a start I can't because I'm writing in English. I'll never be able to write in anything else, I don't even want to. It's an odd position, really, as an English writer coming to live in Israel, because, in a sense, you're an emigrant, and always will be, because your audience is not here, so the position is a bit false in some ways. It's rather like those American writers who went over to France after the First World War – but they were sort of acting up, I'm not acting up or anything like that. They were reviewing their society from a distance, but I'm not, I don't particularly want to go on writing about England. Except it's a bit odd to write books about Israel as an Israeli and to write them in English.' He's right, of course. We'd be like those typesetters with their braille-in-reverse, working with a culture that is recognisable but not properly comprehensible. Without language there'll be neither mastery nor masterpieces. A state of affairs acknowledged by Anton Shammas, Arab author of *Arabesque*, who writes unnaturally in beautiful Hebrew, so I heard it said, because he 'wants to conquer the king's daughter in the king's own palace'. A desire I well understand. Lionel Davidson built his house in Herzliya, but now lives in Hampstead.

2

YEHUDA AMICHAI

In July 1973 I sold a story to *Club International* and, on the proceeds, went to Israel for a month. Just before I left, an old friend said, 'It's funny, but I'll miss you,' and it occurred to me that I would miss her too. I flew out with half a dozen copies of my first novel, *Bibliosexuality*, which had just been published. I presented one to Yehuda Amichai. The visit to his house is described in my story 'The Promised Land', wherein the poet is thinly disguised as A. (though the narrator is not me, of course).

Yes, I am serious. Look at me, I am interviewing A., the famous Israeli writer, for a magazine published by the Hebrew University. At first A. was reluctant to be interviewed without payment, until I told him that I was not being paid either. We are sitting opposite one another, in his living room, sipping tea. No milk, no sugar. Beyond us in the honeydew light the walls of Jerusalem glow. When Jews pray they always face Jerusalem. I bend over my cup and the steam infused with lemon rises like incense. A. has his back to the city. A. is small but not delicate, compact; you'd guess that he was either a poet or a boxer. In his fifties, I'd say. From a generation that has survived wars and worse. Somehow wedded to the land, those that died have become the land of course. He has the dignity of a man whose suffering has not been self-inflicted. Many writers espouse suffering, wear tragedy like a parrot on their shoulder. A.'s poems come straight from the front-line. This is my opinion,

115

not a critical judgment. I switch on the tape-recorder. Questions and answers are recorded. He prefers poetry to prose. He has also led a life of action. In 1948 he ran guns for the Hagganah. Sure, he has risked his life. Now he is secure and famous. He recites a poem for me.

' "Never again will I find rest for my soul"
Let me sit in the revolving chair
of an AA gunner, of a pianist,
of a barber, and I shall turn round and round
restfully until my end.'

The spool of my tape-recorder freewheels, the end of my tape claps. The interview concludes, the baby-sitter arrives. 'Writing a novel,' says A., 'is like starting a marriage – in the beginning you have no idea what you are letting yourself in for.' A. has recently begun a second marriage, the baby-sitter has come to mind the evidence of his continuing creative powers. 'Shalom,' we all say.

A.'s place is in *Yemin Moshe* – the Right Hand of Moses – a higgledy-piggledy grouping of buildings, steps and alleys, the remains of the first modern Jewish settlement outside of the Old City, now being lovingly restored. On a hillside, facing Mount Zion. Beyond it is waste ground leading down to the valley of Gai Hinnon (formerly Gehenna) where children were once sacrificed to Moloch.

Amichai still lives there, or did when I went to see him in April 1986. It is twilight. I am half an hour late, having under-estimated the time it would take to get here from Yosl Bergner's studio in Tel Aviv. Yehuda Amichai is on the street, looking at his house. He is not relaxed. Within, the boy last seen in his cot is watching cartoons on television. He must be thirteen. I do not enquire whether he has had or will ever have a barmitzvah. It is too noisy to talk, so we wander along to Mishkenot Sha'ananim where visiting artists stay. Amichai is a familiar figure there and we are admitted without question. I ask about a book of stories, recently published in America. 'When were they written?' 'In the fifties,' he replies. Then he sneezes. Perhaps that is why he has been tense, waiting for the sneeze. It certainly helps. 'From whose point of view are the stories told?' I ask. 'The narrator is mostly me,' he replies. 'The only motivation I have is to describe the world as I see it.' 'You seem obsessed with impermanence,' I say, 'temporary relationships and habitations in a timeless land.'

As we strolled towards Mishkenot Sha'ananim, Amichai told me that he had been surveying his house, awaiting me, in anticipation of the builders who were soon to add a vertical extension. An odd act of faith, surely, from a man who sees just sand where others see foundations. Perhaps that is why his house has grown so slowly, advancing skywards only when the last gain has been consolidated, never risking the grand gesture that Davidson made. Amichai's eventual aim, I suspect, is to colonise heaven. I leave this addendum to the question unspoken. 'Well, it may be as you say,' he replies, 'but it might well be the other way round. Land and nations, history, are nothing against one single human life. It's a total obsession with time and space. One is measured against the other. When one moves the other moves. Or so it seems. People used to make the mistake of thinking the sun circled around the earth. It's the same here with so much superficial or non-existent movement which only looks like movement.' Perhaps it is more useful to look at a writer's house rather than his prose to deduce his true beliefs.

'Do you think poetry has become more political since the

Lebanese misalliance?' I ask. 'No,' he replies, 'it has always been. I started writing in the early fifties, it was always political in a way. Always war and peace. So I think it's very artificial to say it's political now. Fifty years ago Bialik wrote a lot of political poems, real political poems, expressing his ideas about Zionism and orthodoxy and so on. But he also had others. No, it's not a new thing.' 'How about pessimism?' 'That's also a kind of fashion. Writing about disaster becomes a kind of fashion; to say, Well, we have failed. I don't belong to that school of wailing. I'm too much involved in landscape and real life to be constantly thinking, Ah, what happened to the Israel I knew as a child? It's an old romantic fallacy. It's a very small section of writers and artists who constantly complain, but it was never as beautiful as they describe, and it's not as bad as they think it is now.'

'Do you think you're more Israeli than Jewish?' I ask. 'Well, the settings are Israeli,' he replies. 'Of course I could sit for a year in Oxford and I might come out with a novel about donnish life in Oxford – there are writers who do that – but I cannot, I am too lazy. It needs an effort go out and sit somewhere else. But there is also the midrashic tradition. To take certain facts or happenings and to try to explain them, like commentaries in the holy scriptures or in the Talmud. So I take certain real facts and then thoughts and explanations and commentaries circle around, sometimes reaching very far in a phantasmagorical way, but always going back to the things that really happened. I think this might be a kind of Jewish dialectic. Not so much a dialectic but a way of seeing things. There are certain basic facts in life – life and death and sickness and love and so on – and around them we hang all our ornaments trying to explain them.'

Other writers, whose motivations are less personal, may have begun to undermine national myths, but Amichai is content merely to drop his trousers in public, intending to expose, among other things, his feet of clay. I am referring specifically to an untranslated novel called *Hotel in the Wilderness* after a prophecy of Jeremiah. 'It's a humorous pornographic novel, very pornographic, which the critics didn't like,' explains Amichai, very relaxed now. 'They didn't like it because they like me, so they didn't want me to shatter the image. It was my kind of sweet humorous revenge on all the holy cows, including myself. It's about an old poet who went to America, who hasn't written for twenty, thirty years. A big Hebrew poet in America, who's running a huge factory for women's underwear, takes him in when he's starving to be his advertising man. There's also a scientist who has developed a system for women's buttocks from which he deduces their whole life, like men who explain personality from handwriting. You see its potential. It's actually a big joke on Zionism, on Israel, on religion, on America, on poetry itself and so on.'

'Don't you find the story of the Israelites still has potency?' 'Sure, sure,' he says, 'but it's subconscious, because if it's conscious it's bullshit. The moment it gets conscious it becomes a synagogue, it becomes a rabbi, it becomes a political party and all the other crap, which is totally meaningless. It's a very personal thing. Practising religions are totally meaningless – they are a good way to escape real problems. Real problems? Real existence? We have all kinds of games, whether it's crossing yourself or baptising yourself or jumping into the air or hitting your chest on Yom Kippur or eating matzos for eight days and so on. It's all a big game to keep you busy, which is great. If your main purpose is not to eat bread for eight days you don't have to think about poor people or the problems of the world.' 'Couldn't the same be said of writing?' I ask. 'Sure,' he replies, 'it's the same. But at least I have a free choice, I can either hit my chest on Yom Kippur or cross myself like a Catholic or kneel down like the Moslems do or do all kinds of other games, but I could also write. To me writing and thinking and living with friends and trying to solve problems seems more honourable, also much more dangerous because it's filled with pits and disappointments. If you eat matzos for eight days it makes you feel good, but writing doesn't make you feel good.'

For some reason I continue to fast on Yom Kippur. It has nothing to do with religion and very little to do with sentiment, and it doesn't make me feel good (though I do go to the synagogue for the last ten minutes or so to hear the shofar). It is simply that it would be a sign of weakness not to. Perhaps if I lived in Israel I wouldn't think this way, wouldn't need any marks of solidarity.

Anyway, on 6 October 1973, three months after my first encounter with Amichai, I was reclining on my old bed in my parents' house, killing time till the end of the fast, when a friend came around, and said, 'Have you heard the news? The Egyptians have crossed the canal and the Syrians are trying to cut Israel in two.' That didn't make me feel good either. I cheered up, however, when the friend who said 'I'll miss you' called and invited me to a party in York that same night.

Why not? The shofar blew, I broke my fast, then drove the entire length of the motorway in an autumn fog. I had entered a featureless, timeless zone. But just as I knew that the world behind the mist remained solid, so I also knew that beyond the present, irrelevant moments were the answers to two big questions. Was I on the brink of a romantic attachment? Would Israel survive the night? I sat upon the stairs with Fran smoking dope and talking till morning, except when I arose on the hour to listen to the World Service news bulletins on the kitchen radio. There was no change, everything remained in the balance. But this is not a history book. All I require to conclude this paragraph is a double affirmative: yes, I married Fran, yes, Israel survived. It was a shock though, an intimation of mortality, that was felt even more deeply east of York.

3

SHULAMIT LAPID

Wednesday, 26 February 1986, Cambridge. The girl at the next table in the tea shop is an Israeli, studying English at one of Cambridge's many language schools. When she hears that Shulamit Lapid is sitting a scone's throw away she cries, 'Wow!' An indication that Shulamit is as popular as her husband in her homeland, where she is chairwoman – the first in its sixty-year history – of the Hebrew Writers' Association. What, I wondered, were her responsibilities? 'Well,' she replied, 'its first chairman was Bialik, our poet laureate, so it involves for a start sitting in a very revered chair.' Next comes the welfare of the 400 members, then involvement in social and political issues. 'Adding our voice to good causes.' One of them being the matter of censorship. 'Not only have we taken issue on behalf of the Arab writers in Israel but we demanded the cessation of all censorship on the West Bank. There were about 140 works that were banned. After pressure from us and PEN the list was narrowed down to thirty or forty, all of which they justified to us. For instance, in one case Shylock was compared to a modern Israeli Jew. In a book that purported to be a textbook of Shakespeare for use in Arab schools.'

In fact it was Shulamit's own reaction to such negative stereotyping that drew her to the pioneers of the first wave of immigrants, themselves denigrated by the more articulate, more ideological members of the second aliya, which included Yosl's Uncle Monyeh among its number. They sneered at the farmsteads of their predecessors and called them 'the Baron's settlements', implying that they were all bankrolled by the Montefiores or even the Rothschilds, and in their literature – which is copious – they presented the immigrants as bourgeois idlers who lounged about while Arabs toiled on their behalf. They made one exception from this general condemnation: the Bilu pioneers, who were, on the contrary, regarded as a model worth imitating, which doubtless makes Yosl's present address pleasing to his uncle's ghost. At the heart of this hostility was the question: how did the first aliya change the Jew? Not for the better, said the scribes of the second. In their view this early prototype was as parasitical and as lacking in personal pride as Kafka's jackal.

Probably the most representative and influential of these writers was Josef Chaim Brenner, who settled in Palestine in 1909. *Shekhol ve-Kishalon*, his most famous novel, was the only book Puah Bentovim took with her when she went from Jerusalem to Prague. This is her description of his brief life: 'Brenner, born 1881, Ukraine; murdered, 1921, by Arab riots, despite advocating peaceful collaboration. A very stirring life of a thinker-writer who also tried to be a worker-farmer – writing and workers' politics. In that novel, story of a pioneer who came to Palestine – inner fight between old and new settlements etc. – breakdown, mentally, recovery, back to Europe and back again

– again breakdown. I had no idea as Kafka never uttered his ideas – he didn't want to use German with me – but this book meant more to him than I could ever imagine. Even in Berlin he begged me, with his deep-looking eyes, whether we can continue reading Brenner. But I realised that his new friend, Dora, could absolutely do it, so I asked her both to teach him Hebrew and read him Brenner. Of course I gave it to him as a goodbye present.'

In October 1923 Kafka wrote to Brod that he was reading a little Hebrew, 'chiefly a novel by Brenner. . . . I am not enjoying the book very much as a novel. I have always had a certain awe of Brenner; I don't know exactly why. Imagination and things I have heard were mingled in my feeling about him. There has always been talk of his sadness. And "sadness in Palestine"?' In the letter to Robert Klopstock, dated 25 October 1923, Kafka wrote (just before grumbling that he hadn't seen Puah for a fortnight), 'Now I've been here for a month and have read thirty-two pages of a novel by Brenner, a page every day. The book is entitled *Shekhol ve-Kishalon* – solve that chemical formula. It is difficult for me in every respect, and not very good.'

A clue to Kafka's dislike can be found in the postscript of another letter to Klopstock, dated November 1923. '*Shekhol ve-Kishalon* are two nouns I do not fully understand. At any rate they are an attempt to set down the quintessence of misfortune. *Shekhol* means literally childlessness, so perhaps unfruitfulness, fruitlessness, pointless effort; and *kishalon* means literally: stumble, fall.' Actually *Shekhol ve-Kishalon* is translated as *Loss and Stumble*. Kafka hardly needed to go to Palestine for that, if he wanted to fall Prague and Berlin were handier. Perhaps, after all, the second aliya turned on the first out of self-disgust, just as Monyeh Bergner turned upon himself.

Anyway, it seemed incredible to Shulamit Lapid that all the sufferings of the 'Israeli Mayflower era' had left nothing in the collective memory but the image of 'young ladies playing the piano'. The decisive moment, for her, as for me, was the Yom Kippur War when 'the banana kids, as we were called, the pampered Israelis suddenly became frightened diaspora Jews', as insecure as the first settlers of 1882. Thus she began her first novel, *Gai Oni*, and discovered, not unexpectedly, that all the contemporary dilemmas – Arab against Jew, religious against non-religious, newcomers versus old-timers – were not so new. 'I think the book gives a feeling that we can overcome problems,' she said. 'It happened before, maybe it will happen again.'

Her next novel, *As a Broken Vessel*, was also an exercise in historical rehabilitation; the patient being Moses Wilhelm Shapira, a nineteenth-century dealer in antiquities whose claim to have discovered an ancient scroll of Deuteronomy near the Dead Sea was dismissed by the museums that once lionised him. 'I took all the letters he wrote and sat with a psychologist and we built a character,' she said. 'I went to Germany and found for the first time his photograph. All I had before was a caricature in *Punch* where he was depicted as a very ugly Sturmer-type Jew. His wife, a German deaconess, was described as a beautiful blonde girl. But in Germany I found the portrait of a handsome man with his wife who was an ugly older woman. He was a kind of dybbuk that I slept, ate and lived with for more than three years. Luckily for me and my family the dybbuk went out when I finished.'

There is no doubting the authenticity of the Genizah Fragments in the University Library. Most synagogues had their genizah, a depository for worn-out copies of the sacred texts. The one at the Ben Ezra Synagogue in Old Cairo had strata that began in the seventh century and continued until the nineteenth when the worth of the hoard was finally realised. Now they are in the hands of Dr Stefan Reif, bald like Yossel Birstein, and as adept at conjuring up the dead. He shows us his most prized possession – the signature of Maimonides – and, more mundanely, reads a Hebrew letter written in the twelfth century by an itinerant cantor to his family in Cairo. In particular the homesick chazan describes how much he misses his beloved son. The words, written 800 years ago, move Shulamit Lapid literally; she walks away crying and I recall that her own daughter was recently killed in a car crash. The juxtaposition of the two families, the coincidence of the artless cantor finding words to touch the sophisticated writer, is made even more moving by the medium: the Hebrew language, itself moribund until awakened by Zion. The neutral territory is suddenly a place in which memories come alive, a little Israel. These observations are made after the event because the epistle was read in the original, which of course was lost on me.

We are dining at the University Centre, guests of Dr Risa Domb. Shulamit orders Dover sole. 'Do you want it with prawns?' asks the waitress. 'Without, thank you,' replies Shulamit. The fish is delivered. 'You are kosher?' I ask. 'Not at all,' says Shulamit, 'I thought she asked if I wanted the fish without bones. I love prawns.'

Soon more serious problems of translation are being discussed, as befits the company. Eventually we reach the subject of Shlonsky, poet and translator of Shakespeare into Hebrew. At which point Shulamit tells a story. Shlonsky, it seems, was in London at a big hotel. His wife runs to a friend in the next room. 'Tell me,' she says, 'what is the English for towel?' She says the word in Hebrew of course. 'Why do you want to know such a thing?' asks her friend. 'Because Shlonsky is standing

dripping wet and stark naked in our bathroom without one,'
replies his wife. Here's how I interpret that story. At the
moment Shulamit Lapid herself remains locked in the closet,
clad only in her mother tongue. It's about time we exchanged
clothes.

4

A PROBLEM OF TRANSLATION

Here's another little problem of translation. The basic facts are
taken from the *Jerusalem Post*, dated 21 December 1978. 'The
first bombing yesterday, which injured six, took place when an
explosive charge hidden in a crate was placed at an entrance
serving a restaurant and a butcher shop on David Street, the
main shopping thoroughfare of the market. . . . Ambulances
and security vehicles rushed through the centre of Jerusalem
and were on the scene within minutes of the explosion. The
injured were four Arabs whose names have not been released,
and Miriam Machmouche, and her nineteen-year-old son
Rafi, who were taken to the Hospice Hospital and to Hadassah
Hospital. All the injuries were described as light, a hospital
spokesman said. After security officials searched the area and
questioned witnesses, the market was reopened to traffic.'

It so happens that I walked down David Street with Fran en
route to the Old Yishuv Court in the Jewish Quarter of the Old
City about thirty minutes before the bomb went off. Even

within the thick walls of the museum we hear the echoing thump-thump but think nothing of it, explosions of one sort or another being not uncommon in these districts. Retracing our steps we soon come across the 'security officials' at work, local police with pistols in hand. Then soldiers with guns resting on their hips shout, 'Back, back!' pushing anyone who is not quick enough in their response.

We are now at the intersection of Hajuden and the main street to the Jaffa Gate. It forms a small square, spicy and dusky, surrounded by shops from which dresses hang like unfulfilled dreams, some illuminated by rare shafts of sunlight that slant down from slits in the roof. Outside of each sits the proprietor on a low stool, smoking or reading a newspaper. One, in a grey suit and red keffiych, arises on seeing the soldiers conducting their search and withdraws into his booth, in the shadows of which he picks up an attaché case. He then walks as unobtrusively as possible to a nearby café where he passes the case to another, returning to his seat empty-handed. No one has noticed, except me.

What should I do? Should I tell the soldiers in their flak-jackets? Is he PLO? Or have I completely misinterpreted his actions? Perhaps he is a writer who fears for the safety of his manuscript, or merely a criminal caught with hot money? I can hardly ask him. Nor do the soldiers look as if they have an easy grasp of English. What if they misunderstood me and assume that my Arab actually planted the bomb? Do I want to be responsible for his interrogation? I say nothing.

The street is reopened. We walk past smashed bottles and overturned crates. A man remarks, 'There is no danger. I was in Russia in 1942. Against the Germans these are children playing.'

Had I been fluent in Hebrew there would, of course, have

been no dilemma. Being monolingual, however, I did not dare risk trying to describe an ambiguous situation. And by 1978 the situation was decidedly ambiguous. Menachem Begin, revisionist Zionist, was Prime Minister. Israel had invaded Lebanon in response to a massacre on the Haifa road, the aforementioned Litani Operation. For the first time I felt it circumspect to guess the politics of an acquaintance before voicing an opinion, a circumstance that anticipated the incident at Halhul on the road to Hebron, eight years in the future.

5

SHULAMIT ALONI

When I went to Shulamit Aloni's office on 13 April 1986, a day on which the khamsin blew, her first words to me were, 'Are you going to the demonstration in Hebron tomorrow?' As you know, I tried.

If I were a movie producer casting around for someone to play King David's canniest wife I would look no further than Shulamit Aloni. But I'm just a writer, and she's already head of the Citizens' Rights Movement in the Knesset, in addition to her extra-parliamentary duties with Peace Now. 'What do you stand for?' I asked. In fact she was sitting in a leather chair facing a large desk upon which the world's problems cowered. She laughed. 'The Party stands for peace, for human rights and peace. I established it in '73 to fight for a written constitution and a bill of rights. But once you speak of human rights and self-determination of the individual it means that we do recognise the Palestinian state as an entity. You understand from this that we are dovish. It's very simple and it's very complicated in a country where you have a heterogeneous society, where you have double standards and hypocrisy, where you have people who come from 102 different countries – most of them East European and Middle Eastern – with the psychology of a minority needing safeguards, and being minorities wherever they were they never had responsibility for others because they fought for survival and by-passed the government, so they didn't have responsibility for peace and war, for health, for electricity, whatever you say. We didn't go, the country didn't go through the transformation from this mentality of a minority fighting for safeguards and being the victim, into the situation where we are the majority and we are the government, the legislator, the judge, the police, the army, and it's our responsibility for others. People who do want a democracy but who believe that a democracy is the rule of the majority should know what a majority cannot do, which means to build a system which has checks and balances and a system where the rule of law is above the rule of the majority.'

'Upon what philosophy will you base this law?' I ask. 'Judaism?' 'Everything is Jewish and not Jewish,' she replies. 'Now, why do I say, "Everything is Jewish?" The question is, what kind of Jew do you want to be? I think that the idea of justice, of morality, comes from the Jewish prophets. I think that democracy is very Jewish because we didn't have a Jesus or a Mohammed. According to Judaism every person, man and woman, was at Sinai when the code, the Ten Commandments, was given. It was given to all people, and everyone is responsible for what he does. So it's very Jewish. It's written in Hebrew. And it's very Jewish. And it refers to Israel and it's very Jewish. And the people who have to exercise it are Jewish. So from this point of view it's Jewish. If we believe in history and the dynamic of history the whole idea of Zionism was to bring the Jewish people back to history, because of how they used to live in the diaspora, studying the past and waiting for the Messiah to come – in the present only to survive.'

'Tommy Lapid told me – and I think he was half joking – that the main difference between your parties – both pretty much personal affairs at the moment – was that he loved Jews whereas you were an antisemite. Was he joking?' 'Well,' she replies, 'I am Jewish, my children are Jewish, my husband is Jewish. Don't I love them? It's true that I don't like any group in an abstract way. But how can anyone love a group in an abstract way? Tommy can *say* that he loves Judaism. But I *do*. I think I know Judaism a little more than Tommy Lapid. I studied it. I love it. This is my culture. How can I dislike myself? The question is, what does he understand by Judaism? From my point of view Yehuda Amichai represents Judaism more than one of the clergy who gives you the right to brush your teeth on Saturday. It's true that I fight strongly against making rituals more important than morals and values. I think Judaism gave so much in respect of relations between people, thanks to the prophets who stood very strongly against rituals – the sacrifices and the other things – because they were empty symbols. Like the prophets I believe in values, in everyone having responsibility for his own actions. Everything is in the hands of God except . . . except the belief in God.'

It is a fact that Israel does not have a written constitution because Ben Gurion refused to consider the religious authorities' demand that it be based upon the Talmud, while

130

they, in their turn, refused to countenance any other foundation. Needless to say, Shulamit Aloni stands naturally on the
side of liberal humanism, against the fundamentalism of the
rabbis. In her religion the last word belongs to her, not God. So
what of the future? Like many radicals, Shulamit Aloni paints a
black picture of a land draped in the gaberdines of Poland – if
not the more satanic sartorialism of the far right – but like every
Jew she sees in the end a *goldeneh medina* – which can mean
either a golden land or a fool's paradise. 'Listen! Remember
what I told you about Betar? To them the state is a value, while I
think that it is a means for value, for life, for culture, for human
beings, et cetera, that it's only a kind of instrument. I think that
writers and people who deal with art are very important; those
are the things that stand longer. I'm afraid that since the Likud
came to power in 1977 we are underestimating the importance
of the writer: novelists, poets, playwrights. They write and
create out of involvement because they are part of the life and
they should give – in the way that they can do it – more of
themselves than some of them do. Some of them run away. In
Amos Kenan's novel *The Road to Ein Harod*, on the other
hand, there is the fear that mainly our age group feels – when I
say "our age group" I mean those who fought for the
establishment of the state. As children we – that's my
generation – were the real Israelis, when we grew up we built
Israel. And it was the elite, not everyone participated. And
today we find that this country is running away from us, not
only because of power but because of superstitions and because
of the clergy and because of the destruction of the values we
believed in. We really grew up on the ideas of the prophets, and
a connection between the land and the Bible. And the Bible is
not the book of the religious people – they have the later
writings – the Bible was really the bible of the Zionist

movement, the Zionist revolution of coming back to history, to your land, to your language, to your culture, et cetera. At school I did physics and learned that for every action there is a reaction. And so the more fanatical they become the stronger will be our reaction. I believe a new spirit will come from it.'

Eight days later. Monday, 21 April 1986, London. Amnon Jackont: 'Let's talk of those who believe in the Bible. I believe in the Bible too. I think that our right to the country is really based on the Bible. But, as it happens, I don't believe in the same chapters as the rabbis. They have taken the Bible in a very simplified way. In fact the land was promised because Abraham was a man of values. As a non-religious person, almost a nihilist, I think that I honour the Bible more than they do, because they treat it like a deed. I don't treat it as a deed, I treat it as an elaborate contract between a person and his standards.'

6

AMOS KENAN

Al Saqi Books, London. Amos Kenan has had a nightmare. There has been a military coup in Israel. An anonymous traveller, a leftist, is fleeing for his life. His only ally is Mahmoud, an Arab, also on the run. 'Even in the shadow of annihilation, the eye detects something,' remarks the narrator of *The Road to Ein Harod*. 'Sometimes we would cross an ancient terrace, its stones overgrown with lichen. Lichen is a symbiosis. Algae and fungus feeding on each other. Each gives the other what it has, and takes from the other what it needs. And what would happen if they decided to fight to the death for sole possession of the one stone on which they both live?' The answer is stark: 'Only the naked stone would remain.'

This is a subtle metaphor; by implying that the relationship between Israeli and Palestinian is not only essential but also natural, it makes any dissenting voice sound like that of a self-destructive madman. Of which there are plenty in Israel, though they would not consider themselves such.

Let's translate the metaphor into political terms, which is what Amos Kenan, its inventor, means us to do. In which case we have two states side by side: Israel and Palestine. The latter is anathema to many Jews. This is fair enough, if short-sighted. It ceases to become acceptable when the Palestinians themselves are counted as pariahs or worse. Racism, as we say all the time, is irrational and infectious. To demonstrate just how infectious it can be Kenan tells a little joke.

'In order to join Kach, the party of Kahan, you have to kill two Arabs and a cat. Now the immediate answer of almost everybody is, "Why a cat?" In which case the answer is, "Okay you're accepted." It's a vicious riddle. I tried it on my liberal dove friends in Israel and they also answered, "Why a cat?" It means that back somewhere in their minds killing two Arabs seems more acceptable than a cat.'

Anyway, the fugitives, a Jew and an Arab, are going north, to Ein Harod, the book being *The Road to Ein Harod*. 'Why Ein Harod?' I asked. 'It's a very loaded name,' he replied. 'Ein, in Hebrew, means source, spring, fountain. So the hero of my book wants to go back to the source, to start again. Ein Harod, you see, was the cradle of the dream of a greater kibbutz – an overall thing in which kibbutzim would be the individual cells of a whole organism. And this dream was dreamt in Ein Harod, which is an historical fact. Also, it's the biblical site where Gideon the Judge had the battle against the Midianites and where he chose 300 warriors among thousands, depending upon how they lapped water from the source. It's loaded, also, on the Arab side, because Ein Harod – which the Arabs call Nahr Jalud – is the site of the decisive battle the Arabs had against the Mongol invaders in the twelfth century. It's such a decisive date that they have in the PLO the Jalud Brigade.'

Okay, Kenan seems to be saying, if my metaphors don't convince you, look at the historical facts. The land encompasses two different stories, which are no longer mutually exclusive. Again the choice is stark: corporation or competition. The precedents are not promising. Wherever the fugitives seek sanctuary they hear the echo of an ancient fight. Nor are the prospects pleasing. But Kenan is not without optimism. 'Writing is an optimistic action,' he said. 'Even when you address yourself to the reader in a pessimistic way it is actually an optimistic action.' The fact remains, however, that the possibility of symbiosis is negated in the book by the execution of Mahmoud, and the possibility of renaissance stilled by the final destruction of Ein Harod. Is *The Road to Ein Harod* the writing on the wall? Does it reflect Kenan's fears for the future of Israel?

'It does, and how!' he replied. 'I'm profoundly involved. It's my life. It has been all my life. Of course it reflects my own fears. It's very personal, this book, because it's a message. I want to say something.' He does not, for example, think the idea of a military coup far-fetched. 'It could happen today or yesterday or tomorrow,' he said, 'there are enough candidates for it. It's not a question of who is the candidate. It's the question of a political climate. Let's take the visit of Shimon Peres to England. What did he come for? It's my presumption that he didn't come to make peace. He came here just to avoid war. He cannot deliver peace and nobody knows it better than himself. But to avoid war is as important an action as to make peace. As long as we avoid war there will not be a *coup d'état* in Israel. But the moment that there is a war it will happen, or at least it might happen. It may not even be war but the very grave tension just a second before war which makes the people in Israel feel they need a strong man. Remember what happened before the Six Day War. Then there was a *coup d'état*. Now we know the participants. One of our most dovish doves took part in this *coup d'état*. Maybe that's why he's with the Peace Movement now. And not only him. It's not a coincidence. There is a logic in their change of heart.'

'Is it possible to pinpoint the historical moment when this change took place?' I asked. 'Was it the catastrophe in the Lebanon?'

'I think so,' he replied. 'Lebanon was the greatest disillusion. It was the first time when we lost national cohesion. People who went to the Lebanon went on their own, they were not messengers of the population. And people who lost their children or husbands or fathers in Lebanon belong in Israel to a private club. They don't belong to the nation, the nation ignores them. That's the first time such a thing happens in Israel. This was a war that concerned only its victims, it didn't affect the others. It's a terrible thing to say, but it's also a terrible thing to have happened.'

I am of the opinion that the aforementioned war reopened all the schisms within Judaism that the Holocaust had homogenised, so that the divisions within Israel between left and right, secular and religious are now no less than those between Jew and Arab. I wondered if the symbiosis between Kenan and Al Saqi, an Arab publishing house, was symbolic of this re-alignment.

'Of course,' Kenan replied. 'I can say it openly. There is more affinity between me and the moderate Palestinian than between me and an extremist Zionist.' 'Does the moderate Arab feel the same?' 'Ask him.'

It seems, I said, thinking of Kenan's book, that there is as much chance of war between Israelis as there is of one between Israelis and Arabs. 'There is a latent civil war in Israel and it has been going on for the last few years,' he replied. 'We are two nations in Israel today, and I'm not speaking about the Arabs. Listen, Israel is a strip between the sea and the desert and the whole Bible deals with life in such a corridor. The prophets didn't talk about God but how to adjust to this situation. I think we have to learn this lesson and listen to our ancient prophets and adjust ourselves to live with our environment. If not there will be what is written in my book. I don't want it to happen, but at least I have to make some kind of warning.'

Towards the end of *The Road to Ein Harod* the narrator breaks into the bunker of a crazed general who wants to send missiles through time and space to destroy Israel's past enemies before their dark victories. 'At midnight tonight they'll be blown away,' boasts the tyrant. 'You'll still be alive to see it because you're a pure-blood son of a bitch. Every conqueror has to be sure to keep one representative of the defeated enemy alive so he can testify to his catastrophe for the generations to come. . . . That's why Titus, before he burned the second temple, picked that traitor Joseph ben Mattathias, gave him his dynastic name, Flavius, and made sure he would always have ink in his pen, wine in his flask, food in his larder and a vagina or two in his bed.' The general adds that Flavius was a Cohen, a priest. Not

136

good. In his opinion 'there are no worse sons of bitches than the Cohanim.' Turning to the narrator he observes, 'You look like a Cohen yourself.'

To give further credence to this apocalyptic design the general refers the intruder, his captive, to a work 'by the great military theorist Amos Kenan – a son of a bitch just like you, by the way', thereby associating Kenan with Flavius. I realise that this self-designation is not altogether a joke, so I conclude with this question: 'Let us imagine that peace comes and the twin states of Israel and Palestine flow with milk and honey. What then will the great military theorist and satirist have to write about?' 'I'll write about food,' he replied, 'about how to prepare milk with honey. I've already written a cookbook – it's true – so I'll write another. If that happens I give you a very serious promise that I'll quit journalism and open a small restaurant with only eight tables for the initiated ones.' I don't think any of us need rush to make our reservations.

7

SHIMON PERES

Thursday, 23 January 1986, London. Not reservations but an invitation is what gets me and a few hundred others into a reception at Claridge's for Shimon Peres, in England on a state visit. Brook Street is closed to allow his motorcade to pass unimpeded. Armed police fill every empty space in buildings and between buildings, as though their vigilance at last completed the architect's plans. It is an all-seeing road, reminiscent of the tree that grows outside Yosl's house in Tel Aviv. Perhaps it is a talent specific to certain Jews, that everything they touch sprouts eyes. At first this may seem a blessing, but in the end it is a curse. The police will go home when the party's over, close their eyes and sleep, but that tree, reincarnation of Monyeh Bergner, is always on the alert, so fearful of the future that in the end it will beg the woodman to be merciful and fell it with an axe. Such was the fate of both Monyeh Bergner and Kafka. Shimon Peres is, of course, a more realistic man; he shakes our hands as we enter the reception, but his biggest embrace is reserved not for a prophet but for the apostle of the profit motive, Margaret Thatcher herself. Idealists may spit in their champagne at such an alliance and groan while inanities are exchanged as if they were precious gifts, but such rituals are important; they demonstrate the essential ability of politicians to turn a blind eye.

Afterwards, on the way to the National Theatre to meet my friend Josanne, also on a visit from Israel, I thank the policemen that I pass. You see, I had recently published a novel called *Blood Libels* in which an Israeli politician is assassinated outside just such a hotel. The plot has some relationship to historical events, but in my world everything turns out even worse than in this. Anglo-Jewry is wiped out and there is a military coup in Israel, hence my interest in talking to Amos Kenan. I deliberately set the novel a few years in the past, so as to avoid the adjective 'prophetic', but I am superstitious enough to fear that what I write might indeed come to pass. *The Road to Ein Harod* was meant as a public warning; *Blood Libels* is, more modestly, the expression of my own fears. I have no wish to speak for others, to be a prophet.

8

MOSHE DOR

Sunday, 13 April 1986, The Writers' House, Tel Aviv. The Israeli official who is shot in *Blood Libels* is actually the Cultural Attaché. In fact I had the fate of the former Ambassador, Shlomo Argov, in mind; though not his personality. My Cultural Attaché is a philanderer whose death is as a consequence of this anti-uxorious behaviour. Having written the book I became friends with the real Cultural Attaché, Eli Rosen, and felt obliged to confess what I had done to his fictional counterpart. He was, I think, rather flattered. Meanwhile, in Israel, one of his predecessors, Moshe Dor, published an article in *Ma'ariv*, of which he was literary editor, speculating upon the identity of my model. 'Honest,' I say, 'I made it all up.'

We have been corresponding for some years, but this is our first meeting. Fortunately Moshe Dor doesn't look a bit like Uzi, as described in my book. Moreover, Moshe Dor is a poet, which Uzi certainly wasn't, a man who defines his duties in London with words that were never part of Uzi's vocabulary: 'I thought I was representing the cultural values of the people of Israel, that unique amalgamation of aesthetic and ethical values which is a token of being an Israeli. I tried my best to let those people I was in contact with know that Israel was not only a nation of fighters but a nation of creators and bearers of a message, a very deep inherent moral message carried through the generations.'

In my story 'The Promised Land', the lecherous narrator

139

pursues various Israeli women, hoping to plant his seed in the country's soft and fertile underbelly. At Caesarea with Rivka he thinks he's got it made, especially when she raps upon his door in the middle of the night. He follows her to her room wherein she drops her sheet and reveals her nakedness. But it is only to show my storyteller her sunburn, which he soothes with Nivea cream. 'Such is the role of the diaspora in Israeli life,' he concludes. Moshe Dor, I think, would agree.

'Up to the Six Day War we grew gradually apart from the diaspora. Then came the shock of the war, and the eve of the war when we found ourselves stranded and lonely. The sense of loneliness was horrible and the only ally that we found was the Jewish people abroad. And so we started clinging and then we started drifting away again. The Lebanon War brought us back, but I think that we are facing a certain development which might in the end culminate in the existence of two Jewish entities, an Israeli one and a diaspora one. In the long run I think we will develop certain traits that will be uniquely Israeli and not Jewish in the larger sense. I don't know if it's part of what we call the normalisation of the Jews, because I would have happily given up some of those aspects of normalisation which make us more brutal and mercenary, but it isn't for me to prophesy. You know we have a saying that after the destruction of the second temple the gift of prophecy was given only to babes and imbeciles; one of our great poets – the late Nathan Alterman – in one of his poems dealing with that half-mythical future ends the poem with this metaphor – I quote from memory – "The Shulamit of tomorrow is dressing in her bedroom and we should not try to peep through the keyhole."'

'You say,' I remark, 'that it isn't for you to prophesy. But isn't that exactly what Israeli writers do and exactly what they are expected to do?'

140

'It's certainly true that throughout Hebrew literature commencing with the Bible – if you take the prophets to be our earliest poets and the greatest of them also – you could easily discern the very involved attitude they had with their public. And in some of these beautiful and profound pieces of poetry you can see the very strong, very well-defined moral stands they took concerning the various political and social problems of their day. Now that goes on throughout Hebrew literature, from biblical times until this very day, and I think that this is the main characteristic of Hebrew literature; that sense of responsibility the writer feels. Let's say he's a poet writing lyric poetry which would usually be purely individualistic; even then he remains the mouthpiece of the people, he still carries a certain burden of historical conscience. So if you read a love poem written by a young Israeli during the battle for Beirut you would find within the words, expressions and metaphors and that sense of pain and responsibility I have been talking about.'

It so happens that I have recently been reading just such poetry. Written on scraps of paper, the poems were sent to me at the *Jewish Chronicle* – of which I am the literary editor – by someone called Ramy Ditzanny, a resident of Jerusalem. They were translations from a book of his entitled *From the Ward of the Crippled in Spirit* and were 'inspired', so he informed me, by the Lebanon War. I liked them and printed one called 'My Good Arm' in which a wounded soldier imagines his severed arm flying over a moonstruck city, an arm that 'rolls down nylon tights, feels soft white thighs'. A lyric poem, sure enough, but drenched in sweat, not of love but of fever and fear.

'Thanks for publishing my poem in the Literary Supplement on the 21st December 1984,' wrote Ramy Ditzanny. 'Indeed, I would like to send more; the thing is that I know little about the poetry policy of yours. Last time I sent you poems following the

Lebanon War out of which you chose one. Was it because of its length? Was there political reasoning *vis-à-vis* the issue of the state of Israel as an invader etc. etc. not complying with the general policy of the *Jewish Chronicle*? Myself, I see it as my moral-humane mission to forward-promote this issue, and show the liberal other face of this country (shared by at least forty per cent of the population).' My mission too, as you must have guessed by now.

'Thank you for sketching your literary ethical points of view,' replied Ramy Ditzanny, having read much the same letter I sent my correspondent in Manchester during the affair of Shlomo the giraffe. He also enclosed some more poems of a 'political-liberal-protest' nature. These dropped the fleshy concerns of lyricism altogether and went straight for the bone. I accepted 'Les Enfants du RPG' (RPG being the abbreviation for rocket-propelled grenade), in which a soldier curses a wound inflicted upon him by the eponymous kids, one of whom is lying dead at his feet. At which point I did feel it necessary to impose some minor censorship on behalf of my readers; thus 'the little motherfucker' became 'the little bastard'. It is entirely possible that no one reads my Literary Supplement or, though this is slightly less likely, that all subscribers to the *Jewish Chronicle* are liberal humanists; either way, not a soul complained, or accused me of giving ammunition to the enemy.

This is not always the case in Israel, I gather from Moshe Dor. 'There is no Olympus in Israel,' he says, 'you cannot stay detached from current events, you cannot grow too far from the people. A famous Swiss writer said that everything nowadays is politics, even the smoke escaping from the chimney. In that sense everything is politics in Israel, because of being such a small society and being so close to the sources of public reactions and feelings. As I have said, even in a love poem there is some undercurrent of politics – not necessarily in the sense of actual topical problems, taking a stand either to the left or the right or the centre, but bearing a sort of historic responsibility for the fate of Israel in which our writers have such a direct role to play.' He pauses. Shrugs. 'You have to keep your sense of humour and sense of proportion,' he admits. 'It would also be something of an exaggeration to say that the Israeli people treat writers with such respect and pay heed to whatever they have to say. It's true that because of our traditions we do have a certain reverence for the written word, but I am happy to say, ironically speaking of course, that growing normal now we have shed that respect.'

9

AMOS OZ

In July 1985, when BBC2's *Bookmark* was making its little film about me and my work, Amos Oz happened to be in London for the publication of his own novel *A Perfect Peace*, and, as we knew each other, he agreed to be one of my co-stars. This is part of the script.

> *Interior. Boardroom of publishers Chatto & Windus. Late morning, which makes the bottle of white wine a permissible prop. Also present are the director, Roly Keating, his*

assistant, a cameraman, a soundman, a lighting man and an electrician. The atmosphere is relaxed. Take One.

SINCLAIR: 'Does it bother you that most foreign critics seem to regard you as a politician, a prescriber of Israel's ills, rather than a novelist?'

OZ: 'Well, you know to some extent this may be the destiny of any writer from a small country writing in an esoteric language. I guess a North Korean writing about old age and loneliness would still be expected to deliver some conclusion on the politics in his or her country. Time and again I'm screaming to various interviewers that "No, I'm not a prophet!" But they don't seem to be very impressed, because some of the prophets used this very line. And it is strongly built into the Jewish tradition that writers and poets are expected to be heirs of the prophets – tell the people what to do, where to go, where they have gone wrong. And I find myself struggling with this role – not wanting it, not feeling capable of filling it. History is a nasty nuisance. I know some non-Israeli writers envy us Israelis for having so much history on our hands, for being able to get rid of heroes on the battleground. But history may be a bloody nuisance – you try to write an intimate, low-keyed, local provincial story and suddenly the entire Jewish history is vibrating and echoing in it.'

SINCLAIR: 'Actually, I'm one of those writers who is jealous of your situation.'

OZ: 'Would you like to switch positions for a couple of books, Clive? It would be an interesting deal. I'd buy it.'

SINCLAIR: 'Has being an Israeli ever made you think twice about being a writer? Have you ever exercised self-censorship lest you give ammunition to the enemies of Zion?'

OZ: 'No. I don't give a damn. I sometimes write like the

worst of the antisemites. I can afford it. If I really had to squeeze my entire Zionism into a nutshell it's this: the freedom to be a Jew and write and say whatever I like without giving a hoot about what the others may think.'

SINCLAIR: 'A *Perfect Peace*, your new novel, was in fact begun not long after the Six Day War. Is there any reason why it has taken so many years to complete?'

OZ: 'Well, I started writing it back in 1970 or '71 and after about one hundred pages of manuscript I despaired altogether. I despaired because of the old folks. I had a lot of emotions towards the "lions in winter" in this novel, but I couldn't recollect these emotions in tranquillity. It was only five or six years later – after having been through a nasty car accident – that I could look at these people and listen to them with a certain measure of tranquillity.'

SINCLAIR: 'This leads me to a central relationship in your books: that between fathers and sons, which seems both vital and potentially fatal.'

OZ: 'I would risk a generalisation, Clive. I'd say that almost every young character in my stories requires more than just one father. I would say that living in a country where the founding fathers (and the founding mothers) were much bigger than life, every single offspring of these grotesque giants secretly aspires to adopt a different father. And, by God, many fathers secretly aspire to adopt different sons. This is certainly true of A *Perfect Peace*. Yonatan, its hero, escapes from one father to the next. He never develops the gift for living as an orphan.'

SINCLAIR: 'In several of your books the Arabs are intimately connected with masochistic fantasies of violence. However, these Arabs are not merely "the enemy", they represent the way of life repressed by cultivation – the desert –

the id that is being suppressed by the Jewish superego.'

OZ: 'They represent this and they represent more. In a strange paradoxical sense the founders of modern Israel secretly regarded the Arabs *as the legitimate biblical characters. Consequently, while fighting them they secretly wanted to be like them, they secretly wanted to become as unintellectual, uncomplicated, simple, tough, as the sons of mother earth – of course they have never made it, luckily so. But there remained this secret ambivalence towards the Arabs, a perpetual ambiguity, this combination of fear and attraction, resentment and secret admiration which has to do with a certain aspect of Jewish self-hatred. They wanted to be anything but what they were. I recall the most intimate, endearing nickname my parents had for me was the Yiddish word *shaygets*.

'It took me about twenty or twenty-five years to find out that a *shaygets* is a little Ukrainian peasant boy who herds pigs and throws stones at Jews. Why on earth would my parents, descendants of rabbis and scholars and intellectuals, aspire that their offspring in his turn (that is, little me) should become a *shaygets*, a pig herder, a pogrom maker? Now that's very close to the crux of the matter, Clive.'

SINCLAIR: 'Presumably a perfect peace is unobtainable in this life. It is death, isn't it?'

OZ: 'That's where the quotation comes from by the way, it's from the liturgy, from the burial ceremony. It is part of the prayer said by an open grave – Merciful Lord grant a perfect peace to the soul of . . .'

An imperfect peace. Is that the best Israel can hope for? In 1982, you'll recall, during the second administration of Menachem Begin, the Israeli government launched 'Operation

Peace for Galilee'. It was, in fact, not peace but war; the invasion of the Lebanon to be precise. It was a difficult time for liberal humanists who also happened to be Zionists, not to mention writers who had a pedantic attachment to the meaning of words. I am no historian, but I have opinions; these found their way into my story 'The Last Jewish Joker', and my novel *Blood Libels*, to which this is, as it turns out, a companion volume. My opinions put me in no danger, so far as I know, but in Israel a man with similar beliefs died on account of them.

On 10 February 1983, a couple of days after the Kahan Commission presented its findings on the massacres at Sabra and Shatilla, a young man, Emil Grunzweig, was murdered at a Peace Now demonstration in Jerusalem. A friend of mine, James E. Young, presently a professor at New York University, was there. 'About two thousand of us began to shuffle up Ben Yehuda, chanting for Sharon's resignation,' he wrote in a letter. 'We were surrounded by a throbbing membrane, eight Beginites deep, which moved with us. . . . I linked arms with other Peace Nowniks and we formed a spit-splattered human barricade, which was punched, rammed and cursed – "kibbutznikim sons of bitches!", "fascistim!" Thus we made our way an inch at a time, arms linked, dodging cans and bottles, unable to dodge the spit, launched in leaping thrusts forward . . . the horrible hate in their eyes, their collective snarl, made me sick inside . . . it alternately felt as if something were breaking and then burning. It scared me and made me want to kill them . . . this, I think, because it really seemed that they wanted to kill me, that, if they could, they would.'

Shortly afterwards one of them (it is assumed) threw the grenade that killed Grunzweig. Seven days later Amos Oz addressed a meeting held in his memory.

'From the site of this tragedy,' he said, 'let us issue three appeals: to our Palestinian enemy, to our political rivals in Israel, and to those who share our views.

'First, a few words to the Palestinian people. . . . We have both paid more than enough. Our comrade Emil fought you on the field of battle and returned home to fight to his last breath for reconciliation with you. We call on you, the Palestinians, to turn now to the path of peace, of compromise. Answer our unceasing plea with your own – let us have peace now.

'And a few words to our political rivals at home. . . . Where is this idolatrous fire that you have kindled taking us? Into what abyss is the path you have chosen leading us? What good will it do us to retain the "whole land of Israel", when the soul of the nation is torn in two, when the chasm between us threatens to engulf all that has been built here with the blood and sweat of four generations?

'And finally a word to ourselves. Years ago our fathers used to sing, "We have come to this land to build and be rebuilt." . . . Theirs was a dream we shall never abandon. Never shall we let ourselves answer hatred – no matter from whence it come – with hatred.'

Grunzweig's murder took place in the middle of Israel's cruellest winter. It figures briefly in the Epilogue to Oz's *In the Land of Israel*, grimly turning the metaphorical basis of the book, the explosive atmosphere, into reality. During the preceding autumn, while the Lebanese misadventure rumbled in the background, Oz undertook a journey through Israel, in the course of which he recorded the views of pioneers, zealots, fanatics, fascists, Beginites and Arafatniks. The monologues were initially published in *Davar*, an Israeli journal, at the turn of the year.

A single refrain appears again and again, as if spoken by a chorus: 'What will become of us?' 'What will become of us all, I do not know,' says Oz himself. 'If there is someone with an answer, he would do well to stand up and speak. And he'd better not tarry. The situation is not good.' 'Write that the situation is bad,' echoes a Palestinian in Ramallah. 'The situation?' says a rabbinical student in Jerusalem. 'Not bad, thank God. *M'ken leben*. We're surviving. Nothing to complain about. Thank God for His daily blessings.' Ah, God, who created the Jew to study and the Arab to toil. Some believe that He has promised more than daily blessings. 'Just give us five more years of peace and quiet,' says a settler at Ofra, on the West Bank, 'and the question of the Land of Israel will be sewn up. For good.' No, the situation is not good. The question, already posed by Professor Jonathan Frankel among others, is whether it is permanent.

In giving a voice to his opponents Oz has performed a good deed; he has restored their humanity. He has made hatred harder. In one of the book's many moving passages an Arab journalist describes his first visit to Israel, made in the company of his mother. In a park in Haifa the old lady had suddenly needed a toilet. An Israeli girl was kind to her, and her son wept. 'Perhaps it was my hatred that wept then,' he says, 'because it was dying. My hatred is dead.' But Oz, a writer, also knows that words are not everything. It is not sufficient to *say*, you must also *do*. But again, that chorus, 'What shall we do?' After the victories of 1967 someone told Levi Eshkol, then Prime Minister of Israel, that the finger of God was manifest. Eshkol paused then declared that, if that was so, he was scared. So, too, is Oz.

Or so I thought when I reviewed *In the Land of Israel* for *The Sunday Times*. But scared in print is not necessarily scared in the flesh. These latter-day prophets, these Israeli artists and politicians, have their off-duty moments when they drink beer in the Writers' House, crack jokes, watch television (to which Yosl Bergner is addicted), or flirt with girls. And why should it be otherwise? They are all more or less normal people, and life in the eye of the storm has its calmer moments. No, Amos Oz is not scared, and he can certainly flirt with girls. This is how I recorded our first meeting, in November 1983.

There is at least one little girl in London who, ever after, will love Israelis. Her name is Lucy Owen, daughter of David and Debbie, the latter being the literary agent of Amos Oz. David Owen, my absent host, is a politician. I am, as you know, a writer. In Israel, such distinctions are meaningless. These days, to say 'I am an Israeli' is a political act. To write a book called *In the Land of Israel* is equally political. Yet let no one forget that Amos Oz writes beautiful prose.

So here we are in Limehouse, Lucy and I, awaiting Amos Oz, who is downstairs giving another interview. Although only four, Lucy is already an accomplished hostess, adept at making small talk. Debbie reappears, the Thames flows by the window. 'Mummy,' says Lucy, 'can I have a snuggle with Amos?' At last he enters. He sits in her armchair, she sits on his arm. Lucy, like Israel, is the centre of the world. 'I'd like to sing for you,' he says, 'but I know only Israeli songs. Do you know what a kibbutz is, Lucy? I live on Kibbutz Hulda. Would you like to visit me?' 'I'll have to ask my mother,' says Lucy. 'That's a very diplomatic answer,' says Amos. 'It means you haven't made up your mind yet. Really, would you like to come?' 'I suppose so,' says Lucy.

Downstairs with me, the spoilsport, Oz sings of Israel; half a lament, half a hymn of praise. 'George Steiner says that a Jew owning a national state is like an old man in a kindergarten, that the very concept of a nation state is dangerous, that the Jews should have been above this. Part of me agrees with him. I don't rejoice in having a national state. No one, not Begin nor even the old-timers of the Histadrut, will ever make me rejoice in the attributes of nationhood. I'd love to live in a world where there were a hundred different civilisations, but it is impossible to ignore what has already happened to us. I became a Zionist because of my old grandfather. He was a Russian who had to become a Pole, and then when Poland became independent, he applied for citizenship and was told "no". Although he was a vehement Zionist before Herzl – he wrote love poems for Zion, in Russian of course, and love poems for the Hebrew language, also in Russian – he would never have dreamed of going there. Except no one else would have him. So as long as the bloody name of the bloody game is bars on the windows and locks on the doors and machine guns and passports and presidents, I'll play the bloody game of Zionism from A to Z. It's just that I want, for a change, to be the fifth one in the neighbourhood or the tenth one in the world. However, until the post-territorial, post-chauvinistic era of humanity begins, I'll be an Israeli.'

A couple of weeks before, Edward Said, the handsome Palestinian as Oz is the handsome Israeli, held a seminar at the Institute of Contemporary Arts upon the great unresolved problem of the Middle East. During question time, anticipating this meeting, I asked if there were any message Said might want passed on to Oz. 'Yes,' he said, 'why are there no Arabs on the kibbutzim?'

'It's quite simple,' says Oz, 'they don't want to join. Though, actually, we have one Arab at Hulda. In general, our way of life is totally opposed to their system of values – even the leftists, the radicals, the communists don't like the idea of their wives working in the fields or serving at table.'

Said's point, of course, was that Israel is an exclusive society, whereas his Palestine would be secular, democratic and inclusive. 'Well,' says Oz, 'I think the Palestinian Arabs should be very careful about that. All right, our Law of Return – which gives right of citizenship to any Jew anywhere – is segregationist and racist in their eyes. But the moment they have their state, they will institutionalise their own Law of Return, and they will allow exiled Palestinians to return to their ancestoral lands and they will exclude all other Arabs.' Finally, Oz has his own message for Said. ' "Professor Said," I'd say, "I adore your essays and your articles which I have read. It is a pity they are available in English, but not in Arabic. Let me hear you say these moderate things in your own language to your own people, as I have done in *In the Land of Israel*. This is the major difference between us.'

In the Land of Israel is more than a travel book, more than a report on the nation; it is a celebration of diversity as a writer suddenly discovers the variety of language available to him in his own country. It isn't the Great Israeli Novel, of course, but it is a blueprint, a book of possibilities. 'Perhaps I've tried to make it a substitute for the nineteenth century Russian family saga. A large, troubled, divided family. But to hear all those jargons was a joy, a storyteller's joy.'

But, being Israel, there was more to learn than that. At Bet Shemesh, Oz heard the complaints of the North African Jews. And what has he learned? And what is to be done?

First, the idea of the melting pot – so innocently cruel – has had its day. North Africans can't be Polish Jews. Besides: 'Israel is not going to turn more Western; it's going to become more Mediterranean, more passionate, more angry, more verbally violent. Herzl's vision to transplant a kind of Austro-Hungarian state was sheer lunacy. Once our quarrel with the Arabs is settled – as it must be, no conflict is eternal – Israel will become a kind of Jewish Greece, whether the European Jews like it or not. Meanwhile, the Arabs are becoming more Jewish. You

152

know, the PLO has taken on many of the characteristics of pre-statehood Zionism. Let me tell you, sometimes I feel more of a gut solidarity with Palestinians like the journalists on *The Arab Dawn* than I do with those infuriating ultra-orthodox, anti-Zionist religious fanatics. We speak the same language, we use the same vocabulary. In a sense, whether we like it or we don't, we have made the Palestinians part of the Jewish family.' Part, therefore, of *In the Land of Israel*.

So I ask Oz: Who is the real enemy of Israel, the Arabs or the anti-Zionist Jews or the zealots of Gush Emunim? 'We are reaching the moment of truth,' replies Oz. 'What is it we want? The answer is becoming more and more urgent. What is a Jew? What is an Israeli? What is a Palestinian? What is the name of the game? Is it normalisation? Is it the religious-secular dialectic? Whatever the answer, one thing is certain. We Israelis are on the stage, we are the drama, though whether it is a good or bad performance is not for me to judge. Diaspora Jewish intellectuals may be first-rate critics, but they are involved in a third-rate drama. No, only in Israel can there be collective Jewish creativity. Listen, Clive, for God's sake, next time you are in Israel, go to Ashdod. It's a nice, pleasant, humane city. It's what we are, or what we can be.' Oz has raised Ashdod above Jerusalem, Paris, Vienna, Prague, Warsaw or Cracow precisely because 'she is all we have that is our own . . . she is not quite the grandiose fulfilment of the vision of the prophets and the dream of generations; not quite a world première, but simply a city on a human scale.'

10

DOV YERMIYA

I was in Israel next in June 1984 when, instead of going to Ashdod, I spoke to as many people as I could in Tel Aviv and Jerusalem about the approaching election. Jesaja Weinberg, you'll recall, feared that Israel might become 'fascistic' if Marach – the Labour alignment – didn't win. It was a prevailing fear that gave me the idea for the military coup in *Blood Libels*.

I also arranged a meeting, in the interests of that novel, with an old soldier, Dov Yermiya, who had fought with Wingate in Palestine, the general not the soccer team. Now the language of football, as everyone knows, is full of military metaphors – 'attack', 'defend', 'shoot', – so it was inevitable, when I took up writing about Israel, that I would move away from the playful pursuit of metaphor in the direction of the thing itself; the birth of the nation, when 'shoot' simply meant what it said. I felt, therefore, that if I was going to write about Wingate Football Club in *Blood Libels*, I needed also to consider the man who inspired it. If my writing has any consistency it is that I like to take things to their logical conclusions.

I first saw Dov Yermiya sitting at the foot of the Montefiore Windmill in Jerusalem. He is a man who once, in a happier time, could have passed as the personification of Israel. His sunburned face was friendly, notwithstanding his steely grey hair and a fierce white moustache. His shirt, of course, was open at the neck. He wore jeans and leather sandals, and looked younger than his seventy years. We walked away from the Windmill, which had proved useful as a lookout in the War of

154

Independence, toward Dor Vedorshav and the coolness of an Arab villa, now converted into apartments.

'So you want to know about Wingate, and how I happened to be at Kibbutz Hanita on the night that brought him fame all over the country?' he asked. His stories, which took Wingate from Hanita to Ein Harod – scene, you'll recall, of Gideon's triumph and Kenan's nightmare – found their way – altered only slightly to conform to the conventions of fiction – into *Blood Libels*, wherein Dov Yermiya became Dov Yemina.

In the novel, I regret to say, he is done away with by a right-wing death squad. Since Shimon Peres became Prime Minister by the skin of his teeth (as a result of that '84 election) such prognostications have seemed more like paranoid fantasies than accurate prophecies (though by the time you read this there is no knowing who'll be Prime Minister, and what the atmosphere will be like). But even in the days of Shimon the Good it happened – and was photographed by the Israeli press – that Dov Yermiya was dragged away from a demonstration by the civil authorities, with whom he is not popular. The reason for his unpopularity in those quarters emerged when he told me things about a more recent war I would rather not have known. Dov Yermiya was, I discovered, an unwilling expert on the Lebanon, having been there both in 1978 and 1982.

'For the last fifteen years,' he said, 'since I was discharged from the reserves because of my age, I have been a volunteer. I'm a Lieutenant Colonel by rank, and I know Arabic, so I have been attached to a military government unit that prepares itself in case of war to go after the fighting troops and take over the tasks of the civilian authorities. Of course in the war the title "military government" was erased from our name because we didn't fight the Lebanese, as you know. Instead they called us the Unit for Help to the Civilian Population. I had an important job. I was in charge of services like water, electricity, medical supplies and so on.

'You understand, I opposed the war from the beginning, even before the beginning. The week before it started we had a meeting in a kibbutz called Misgab'am that had been recently hit by the PLO. There are good boys there who were very active in opposing this war and we tried to prepare a demonstration by inhabitants of Galilee, but we didn't manage to finish the organisation because we were called to the banner, as they say. I went because I was sure that I could do the job of helping the victims of the war better than anyone else, or at least I wanted to. That's why I held on although I knew that the army – the government certainly – was making a big error and that my unit wouldn't be much better. And I was right, so I decided, this time I'm not going to keep calm, this time I will write down every detail and publish it afterwards: the terrible bombardment, the shelling, the killing and the destruction which was sheer brutality, sheer vandalism. I saw many dreadful things. I saw the torture of prisoners. And every night I wrote a new page.'

It took Yermiya a year to get his Diary in print. No 'honourable' publishing house would touch it. Only in March 1983 did it appear, under his own name, without the benefit of military censorship. As a consequence Yermiya was retired from his unit; though cause and effect must be deduced as Yermiya has never had an official explanation. It was published in England as *My War Diary* by Pluto, a left-wing publishing house not renowned for its pro-Israel sympathies, which enabled some to dismiss it unread as yet another squib from the anti-Zionists. On the contrary, Yermiya is a Zionist who has seen his ideal of peaceful co-existence hijacked by the Revisionists (whom he refers to only as 'they' or 'them') in the name of Greater Israel. His idealism, it should be added, is no

156

theoretical dream based upon a romantic conception of the Arab, but rather upon the practical considerations of a soldier who has been forced all his life to count the Arabs as the enemy, but has never precluded the possibility of friendship with those he has met or ever lost respect for the humanity of those he doesn't yet know. Seeing the Israeli soldiers encouraged to cast this respect aside persuaded Yermiya that it was time to break silence and risk 'giving ammunition to the enemy'.

From the outset Yermiya watched his efforts at amelioration blocked by his own commander, whose credo was, 'They shouldn't be helped. Let them starve. Let them run.' 'I write in my book,' Yermiya said, 'that on 18 June 1982 we had a meeting of the senior officers of the unit which was also attended by Minister Meridor, whose role was Co-ordinator of Activities for Aid and Restoration of the War Refugees. He came to us as a higher authority to hear what we are doing and to tell us what he is thinking about it. He said how to handle the Lebanese population, and he was quite generous about them, generous in mouth. Then somebody said, "What about the Palestinian refugees? There are tens of thousands of them." His immediate reply was, "Let them go east. Push them as much as you can. Do everything that they can't come back." I wrote it down on the spot, because I wanted to be exact. It is in the book. A friend of mine, a member of the Knesset, to whom all the time I sent material saying that something terrible is going on up here, raised a question: "What has Minister Meridor to say about Yermiya's story?" He replied, "I need not answer this psychiatrically disturbed person."' Yermiya refused to accept his Operation Peace for Galilee ribbon, but will proudly wear his 'psychotic' decoration until the end of his days.

'From the beginning,' he said, 'I was trying to bring my war to anyone who would listen. After my first tour of duty I met with

157

the central committee of Mapam and with Shulamit Aloni; I
went to the kibbutzim and gave lectures. I tried to raise hell but,
you know, in Israel nowadays you can bark to the moon but *they*
are having their way. Then, when I understood that I would not
be seeing any more service in the army, I went to see my
comrades in the Jewish-Arab Circle for Friendship in Western
Galilee. On the basis of this Circle we have established a
committee for humanitarian help for the Palestinian refugees
in Lebanon. We collected seventy tons of food and clothing,
but we were not allowed to take it over the border. Then after
three months something changed, especially the weather. Our
government feared there would be a catastrophe and we were let
in. We met the refugees at Ein El-Hilwe who told us they
would rather have something done for their school. They asked
us if we could bring some prefabs to replace the school that was
razed to the ground. So we started to collect money. We
managed to collect more than $50,000 which for Israel is a lot.
In July '83 we delivered the last buildings. By that time it was
starting to get a little bit risky to go there because the shootings
were starting. We were ready to go on but the authorities said,
"It is too dangerous to endanger Jewish lives for the sake of those
bastards, and anyway we have done enough for them." They
said *we* not *you*. They were impudent enough to publish that
the help came from the Israeli government! The more bright
part of it is that about two months ago I got a message that in the
school we delivered there are now one thousand pupils to learn
there and that it is being used in the spirit we intended.' I last see
Dov Yermiya walking quickly down the street, brief-case in
hand, en route to yet another political meeting. No need to
enquire which side he's on.

11

PARTY PROPAGANDA

The previous night Yosl Bergner, the well-known television addict, had telephoned me at my temporary Dor Vedorshav address to remind me to turn on in time for the 'party propaganda'. There were no actual programmes being shown because of a strike, but the courts had ordered an exception to be made for the political broadcasts. So at 21.30 the blank screen came to life. I understood few of the words, but the images were eloquent enough. Marach begins with a hitch-hiker for whom no one stops. He tells a sad story. The film freezes on his face. More faces in a variety of shades and ages all singing the party song – *Marach Hatikva*, 'Labour the Hope'. It concludes with ex-president Yitzhak Navon in an open-neck shirt. He is quiet but passionate and obviously sincere, the man to soothe the nation's wounds.

Likud is full of Yitzhak Shamir in a natty suit that means business. No less apparent is the national flag. The background is filled with marching songs from the days of the Palmach, the underground army, in the hope that patriotism will anaes-thetise the memory of more recent military fiascos and 400 per cent inflation. The *National Religious Party* compares candle-light to disco lights, a shabbat bride to a teenager with the morals of an alley cat. The final image is of a vase of flowers being smashed. Then Marach reveals the cost of inflation, while Likud shows its pride in Israeli high-tech. Tehiya regards even Herutniks as dangerously pink. Its commercial is full of romance, cross-cutting images of Israel's pioneers with the new

159

heroes of Gush Emunim. In conclusion Geula Cohen, the right's La Passionara, makes an emotional speech and flags wave like mad.

The campaigns worry me. Marach seems to have nothing to set against the confident use of nationalistic imagery as deployed by Likud and its cohorts. Amnon Jackont puts it thus: 'Marach cannot compete with the propaganda effect of the right. How can you sell doubt? How can you persuade people to be doubtful without it being destructive for them? It's very difficult, it's like selling invisible water.'

12

JOSHUA SOBOL

Some, however, claim there is no difference between the parties. For example, Samih al-Qasim, the Palestinian poet resident in Israel, who said as much at a conference on censorship called 'They Shoot Writers, Don't They?', held over a spring weekend in 1984 at the Institute of Contemporary Arts. Also billed to attend was Joshua Sobol, the Israeli dramatist, though in the end he didn't. By way of compensation here is a short dialogue we performed in Tel Aviv shortly thereafter. I began by quoting Samih al-Qasim. 'Are the parties really the same?' I asked.

SOBOL: 'No, I think there is a diffference. The Likud stem

from Jabotinsky. He was a brilliant man, but for him manifestation was more important than being, if you take it philosophically. He was a man who loved all kinds of pomp. Begin inherited it from him. Whereas Marach belong to a very pragmatic tradition in the Zionist movement. I thought I was going to vote Marach until they came out with large advertisements in the newspapers which said, No to a Palestinian State, No to a dialogue with the PLO, No to a return to the 1967 borders, only Yes to a Jewish State. Well, the moment they say this I cannot vote for them. They don't know what to do with the Palestinian problem because they lack the courage to say that the Palestinian people has a right to independence. But because they are such pragmatists they understand we cannot afford to go on as we have been doing. A government led by Marach in coalition with the smaller dovish parties, my preference, would stop the hysterical activity with the settlements in the territories. This is the great difference for me.'

SINCLAIR: 'At the same session Samih al-Qasim, forming an alliance between leftist Jews and Arabs for public consumption, claimed that you also had been censored. I understood differently, but didn't want to contradict him until I had spoken to you. Have you?'

SOBOL: 'Well, they sent a committee of censors to see *Soul of a Jew* and they decided not to cut it. Later we had a problem at a small theatre here in Tel Aviv where I put on a satirical play. The censors tried to ban it. There was a scandal. So they sent a committee to see the show again and they decided not to ban it after all. They were not brave enough to do it probably. I think it's mainly the Arab writers who suffer from the effects of censorship.'

SINCLAIR: 'Can you see yourself ever becoming a dissident

writer? Perhaps in a certain amount of danger?'

SOBOL: 'It might happen. I can give you the scenario. If the Likud together with the right-wing parties take over and they rehabilitate the Jewish underground – give them an amnesty – I think that then the deeds of the terrorists will become a norm in Israel. By the way, I'm almost sure that the Israeli government knew of these deeds – I mean they knew who perpetrated them. In that case I think that the situation might develop into one where even Israeli leftists or dovish personalities might be persecuted.'

SINCLAIR: 'By the government or by terrorists?'

SOBOL: 'By extremists backed up by the government.'

SINCLAIR: 'Your latest play about the last days of the Vilna ghetto recently opened in Haifa. I remember when I published an extract from it in the *Jewish Chronicle* Literary Supplement I wondered if there would be any adverse reaction. How did the critics respond to *Ghetto* here?'

SOBOL: 'They liked it, but there was only one critic who really referred to the implications of the play for the present Israeli situation. That was Boaz Evron of *Yediot Aharonot*. He said it dealt with the question of how we – Israelis – have been influenced in a very strange way by Nazi ideology, by its egoistic nationalism. He thought that this was the main issue of the play for an Israeli audience, and stated that the question was so important for us nowadays that it should be put on the table.'

SINCLAIR: 'Why not write directly about contemporary Israel?'

SOBOL: 'Because I think that if we want to understand what is happening in Israel today we have to go to the past and try to see where are the roots of it all. You know, when I wrote the play one of the things I found was an article written by

Martin Buber in November 1939, a year after *Kristallnacht*. It seems that at that time there were Revisionists in the Zionist movement who said that the Nazi ideology in itself is not bad, that it is almost the most effective ideology for a nation in a state of crisis. What was bad about the Nazi ideology, of course, was that it was directed against Jews. Apart from that unfortunate perversion they shared its belief in a policy based on national egoism. And Buber says in his article that this is the most terrible abomination he knows of assimilation, and he goes on to say that if a day comes when we adopt Hitler's god here in Palestine and only change its name into a Hebrew one then we are lost.'

SINCLAIR: 'So Israel is a continuation of diaspora history?'

SOBOL: 'Yes it is, but in a very distorted way. What I tried to show in *Ghetto* was that the Jews in Vilna tried to resist the Nazis, not by using force against them, but by resisting spiritually and morally, by trying to survive not only as living creatures but mainly as human creatures. They wanted to survive and come out of this terrible hell as human beings. I think that's why they made the theatre and that's why they created the library and had all the cultural activity in the ghetto. For years this was not mentioned here in Israel. The consensus was that most of the people went as sheep to the slaughter, whilst there was a minority of heroes who stood up and resisted the Nazis gun in hand. Well, what I found out while making my research for the play was that resistance in the ghetto represented a very small minority, less than one per cent of the population. The best people, I think, were involved in this kind of moral and cultural surviving.'

SINCLAIR: 'Did any survivors see *Ghetto*?'

SOBOL: 'That's exactly what I want to tell you. The theatre invited survivors of two kinds, if I can put it that way; some were in the partisans and others were just survivors. Those who were in the resistance movement attacked the play, some of them. They said the play ignored the fact of the resistance in the ghetto by putting a very strong emphasis on the Jews who just survived. They asked me, what do you want to do with the play, what kind of example do you set for youth? Then there were those who just survived. They came out with a very fierce attack on this tradition of glorifying the resistance and ignoring totally the fact the majority were just survivors – second-class survivors, they called themselves. They said they felt for the first time that justice was done to them and to their way of living through the Holocaust. It was very, very interesting and Israeli television tried to make something of it. In one of the meetings a woman came out with such an attack on the tradition of praising the armed resistance and ignoring the rest of them that everyone around started weeping. They couldn't go on. Filming stopped. They didn't want to show such grief on television. And this was one of the strongest moments of the whole symposium. Well, there was censorship, but of another kind, benign censorship.'

SINCLAIR: 'It's ironic, isn't it, that the culture they were trying to salvage was more Western European than Jewish?'

SOBOL: 'You are absolutely right that they were not trying to perpetuate the Jewish orthodox tradition. Those who were, let's say, Bundists believed in universal humanistic values, and that's what they tried to save. If you take the ghetto of Vilna I think that the most active people came from this non-religious tradition.'

SINCLAIR: 'So, in one sense, the Zionist tradition isn't Jewish at all?'

SOBOL: 'That's why I think there's a contradiction between

Zionism and orthodox Judaism. Nowadays in Israel they try to make a whole mixture, a mishmash of Zionism and messianism. I don't think that Zionism had anything to do with messianism originally. It was, as you said, a secular ideology, a nationalistic ideology, trying to re-implant the Jews in an historical context. It's only after the Six Day War that messianism all of a sudden started to become the expression both of Judaism and of Zionism and I think that this is our worst catastrophe.'

SINCLAIR: 'But what was the alternative to winning?'

SOBOL: 'Since there was a war we had to win it, but the outcome could be different. Immediately after the war we could have started to negotiate with the Palestinians, have offered them a solution. We could have offered them national independence at that time. I think that the moment this was not done we lost everything. That failure made us what we are now: a colonialistic society.'

Again, Sobol hardly looks the gloomy soul his opinions would indicate. We are in fact drinking cold beer in his apartment on Melchett Street, Tel Aviv, accompanied by Edna, his wife, Gedalya Besser, his director, and numerous kids; in other words an optimistic spirit prevails. Indeed, there is much excitement as the group is off to Berlin on the morrow for the German première of *Ghetto*, and much speculation about how it will be received. Somebody remarks that one of the younger geniuses of the German theatre said, on being introduced to an Israeli, 'Now I know what it is like to meet someone who has cancer.'

13

OTTO WEININGER

This reminds me of the words Sobol put into the mouth of Otto Weininger, the central character in *Soul of a Jew*: 'Do I have some contagious disease, or some condition that people are ashamed of?' The answer being yes; the disease being Jewishness. For Weininger, prodigious philosopher of *fin de siècle* Vienna, was a passionate Jew-hater. It was his bad luck that he was also a Jew, which did little for his self-esteem. Nevertheless, he wrote one book, *Sex and Character*, with which he hoped to alter the consciousness of mankind (only mankind, he loathed women nearly as much as Jews). Weininger argued that Aryan masculinity was the paragon which would redeem humanity, representing creativity, meaning and infinity. Judaism was its enemy, being the 'very antithesis of masculinity'. Weininger sneered at Zionism, prophesying that Herzl's experiment would be 'engulfed in the abyss of Judaism'. Kafka, of course, partook of Weininger's self-hatred, but with one essential difference: he didn't think he was Jewish enough, and felt that a new life in the Promised Land might just turn him into a whole man. In short, he believed that the Jew had been poisoned by Europe. Weininger believed the opposite; he was convinced that Judaism had corrupted Europe.

Sobol regards Weininger as a man who couldn't accept his identity, but who couldn't escape it either, his Jewishness being too firmly embedded in his character to be dislodged by a symbolic conversion to Protestantism. In *Soul of a Jew* Weininger's best friend becomes a Zionist for the most

Freudian of reasons: to attract a woman. Clara, the woman in question, is Weininger's true foil. Her Zionism is a version of existentialism, being based upon the belief that the Jews, to absolve themselves of guilt, should return to the place where they first brought ruin upon themselves: 'that's where we have to start all over again and we'll try to avoid the mistakes that caused our downfall.' Israelis, says Sobol, reworking Clara's speech, must become a special type of existentialist and be prepared to bear the burden of their actions, hence his emphasis on 1967 as a turning point, a lost opportunity for redemption. I wish them luck in Germany, that redeemed land.

It turns out that not only *Ghetto* but also *The Night of Weininger* (as the Germans call it) are big successes, so much so that productions of the latter move from city to city. Fred Weininger, an artist and poet domiciled in Israel, is in Hamburg to represent Yiddish writers at the International PEN Congress. His eye catches sight of a poster advertising *The Night of Weininger*, and he wonders whose night it will be: his cursed ancestor's or his own. He enters the theatre. By the time he leaves his heart is raging. 'Restlessness and anger boiled in me. . . .' he wrote in *Ma'ariv* on his return. 'I was ashamed of belonging to the human race. I returned to the hotel beaten and humiliated. Is it possible that the lowest in man can get lower still? Joshua Sobol, I accuse you of treachery, of selling Jewish blood and flesh to a world which is upset at the fact that we are still alive and to gullible Israelis who would willingly shake off the name Jew, if this were made feasible for them, and who believe that you reach the apex of your self-expression in this form of art. And what of the gentiles who consciously or unconsciously would identify with this anti-Jew Otto Weininger, and would derive pleasure from this form of legitimate antisemitism? Legitimate, for it came not from the

167

pen of Fassbinder, but from one whose name is Joshua Sobol –
"*Auch ein Jude.*" He is also a Jew, as two Germans said to each
other while reading the poster outside the theatre. The price of
the Jew is cheap at a time when the ground of Auschwitz is still
moving with the convulsions of the war for survival our martyrs
fought there.'

These are serious charges, which I would answer by
reminding Mr Weininger Jr that Sobol is also an Israeli, and as
such is entitled to ask why the country no longer meets his
requirements.

At which point, ladies and gentlemen of the jury, I should
like to call a surprise witness for the defence: Otto Weininger
himself. Apparently, just before the première of *Soul of a Jew* in
Haifa, Sobol, Besser and Doron Tavori, the leading actor,
consulted a spiritualist who, aided by a Ouija board, made
contact with the unquiet shades, one of whom spelled out his
name in Hebrew: Otto W. Note the language; had Weininger
whiled away the first part of eternity with a Hebrew primer in
order to become, albeit posthumously, a better Jew? Otto, are
you happy being impersonated on stage? 'Yes.' What message
do you want to get across to your Israeli audience? 'Emergency
exit.' Otto, what do we have to do to understand you? 'Die.'
Will we be better off dead? 'No.' His disposition, it seems, has
not been improved by being dead, despite the fact that death
was his choice.

Like Monyeh Bergner he shot himself in Vienna, and like
Monyeh Bergner he was a while dying. Nor have his spirits
been raised by turning up in Israel with the lingo already to
heart. Which leads us, ladies and gentlemen, to the big
question: is it really possible to do anything for the self-hating
Jew who is, after all, a pretty representative type? Is there a cure
for the diaspora blues? Is Israel it? Let us call up Monyeh

Bergner on what passes for my Ouija board. Monyeh, why did you do it? 'What?' Leave Israel. ' "Never again will I find rest for my soul." Not even there.' So why did you shoot yourself? 'The ground was crumbling beneath my feet. Here, there, it made no difference. The feet were the same. Those damn boots from Galicia.' Now Kafka. Franz, do you really think you would have been a different man in Israel? 'Only a different man could have gone in the first place.' But plenty of Jews did go. 'Plenty of Jews also went to Balaban's retreat, much good it did any of them.' Who's Balaban?

14

AHARON APPELFELD

In order to attract residents to his so-called Institute of Advanced Studies Balaban, a former horse-trader, promises 'that within a short space of time he would painlessly eradicate embarrassing Jewish gestures and ugly accents'. This miraculous metamorphosis will be accomplished, Balaban believes, as a consequence of 'horse-riding, swimming, seasonal hunting, organised hikes and what he called assimilation into the countryside'. His ambition is to ensure that no Jew will have to be ashamed any more, not Franz Kafka nor even Otto Weininger.

Although the location is Europe and the year 1938, it is difficult not to feel an unspecific timelessness, especially if you happen to be travelling from Tel Aviv to Jerusalem, on a road that mimics the route to the sanctuary, in the direction of Aharon Appelfeld's home at Mevasseret Zion. For Balaban's attempt at bucolic assimilation, as described in Appelfeld's novel *The Retreat*, is surely a marvellously subtle compression of both emancipation and Zionism.

Certainly when Appelfeld himself reached Palestine in 1946 at the age of fourteen, having escaped from a concentration camp and lived for three years in the Ukrainian backwoods, he too underwent a form of indoctrination, 'an Israeli one'. 'Like all big movements,' continues Appelfeld, 'Zionism was utopic, saying: "We are going to change the Jew, we are going to change the world." My teachers believed they were creating a new generation, a new type of sabra, blonde, big and high; would-be peasants, beautiful and strong. But this was just an illusion, wishful thinking. How can you change people, a nation, a character? – it's unchangeable.'

Not surprisingly, Appelfeld maintains that his roots remain in Eastern Europe, the subject matter of his best novels. That being so he asks the following question: 'What does it mean that you are an Israeli?' And answers himself thus: 'I think that this is still a country of immigration. True, if you are living here it means a kind of commitment to Jewish history, the Jewish issue. But I can imagine myself sitting in London and still being committed to Jewishness. I could never count myself as an Israeli writer. I would not easily say this sentence, because it is a very tragic sentence. Don't forget that just fifty years ago Europe was the centre of Jewishness, physically and spiritually.'

'Why then,' I say, 'don't you write in German?' 'I was born in a town near Czernowitz,' replies Appelfeld. 'It was, I would say, a nest of many famous German writers – the most famous of course is Paul Celan – a breeding ground for German-Jewish writers. So there was somewhere a temptation even for me to become a German writer. But see how tragic it would be that I, a victim of the Germans, should write in the language of the murderers – it would be more than irony, more than irony. Even if I had chosen this, some way Hebrew became my mother language, thank God – don't forget I never attended school as a young person before I came here. There is another point, that I created for my heroes, even for the assimilated ones, I created a Jewish ground for them.'

'Wouldn't they be surprised, though, to find themselves speaking perfect Hebrew?' I ask. 'Doesn't it add an overlay of irony to your fiction? You've turned assimilated German-speaking Jews, doomed Jews, posthumously back into real Jews.' 'Let me put it another way,' replies Appelfeld, 'they have been forced to be Jewish by an outside force. And by me forced again to be Jewish. They were hated in the environment they created, maybe in my environment it's a bit softer. I'm not going to deny their deep assimilation, even their hatred of themselves. It's a Jewish phenomenon, you cannot deny it, it cannot be hidden, it's a part of Jewish fate.'

It should be added, yet again, that the fatalism conveyed by these words is considerably mitigated by the atmosphere in Appelfeld's own home, which he shares with his wife and their three vivacious children. Moreover, during the course of our conversation Appelfeld took me through his back garden, where he picked me a peach from his own tree, and pointed across the valley to the next hill. The cairn of stones on top of the promontory is really the ruins of a fort, explained Appelfeld, hence its name, Castel. Appelfeld outlines its recent, heroic history: how, in 1948, it commanded the road to Jerusalem, how, with many losses, the Israelis took it from the Arabs.

Pursuing the connection between Balaban's retreat and

Appelfeld's newish country, I wonder if the divisions exposed by the Lebanese misadventure aren't the same controversies that provide Appelfeld's own novels with their intellectual background. 'They are coming alive,' says Appelfeld, 'they are happening again. But with the experience of the Second World War behind us. The scenario is very similar. We are surrounded by many countries that want to kill us. But today we have an army, tanks, with all their dangers.' Like most Israeli intellectuals Appelfeld speaks of Sharon as 'the crazy one', but he adds this: 'My feeling is – correct me if I am wrong – that in England and in Germany they were waiting for many years for a Lebanon War. Because, you see, after the Holocaust it was not fashionable to be an antisemite. But now it's wonderful for them. They have the image of Sharon with his heavy stomach, and confirmation that the victim is no more the victim. The victim is just a mask. Beneath he's satanic. I was very excited by the antisemitic press in Britain, which is why I like to compare what happens here to what happened in the Falklands. You had in Lebanon an international terrorist nation in the making. Supported by Russians to create an Arab-Russian communist state against us. Then you have the Falklands – somewhere in the South Atlantic. I was very interested to see how suddenly your newspapers became patriotic. You have to compare them with the newspapers here. I give you now a good reason to learn Hebrew, Clive. It is to read these newspapers, to see their sometimes masochistic overcriticism. It is very Jewish. And I'm very happy that it is so. I could not stand it if it were different. So, thank God, we still have this kind of element: sceptical, critical, overcritical, and so on.'

Finally, I think, Appelfeld sees Israel as 'the accumulation of all the Jewish elements in one small spot – concentrated'. The perfect location for a writer who permanently explores Jewishness. 'I'm constantly writing about the present,' he says, 'even if I'm writing of the past. I have never been interested in the sociological novel or issues. I'm interested in Jews, and they will probably be the same Jews no matter where they are located.'

'Doesn't the fact that you are writing about them in Hebrew make a difference?' I ask. 'I'm writing mainly about people who were immigrants,' replies Appelfeld. 'They were smugglers in Europe, they continue to be smugglers here. They were prostitutes in Europe, they continue to be prostitutes here. They were restless there, they are restless here. They were not traditionally Jewish, but traditionally assimilated. The miracle is that only in my books are they speaking Hebrew. So, I'm writing a lot about Israel, but mainly about rootless people who are living in two cultures, two dimensions – the snow from one side, the sun from the other.'

Appelfeld laughs, then describes the sad experience of some writers who have indeed come from the snow into the sun. 'In Eastern Europe they were someones,' he says. 'Here they've not even got a language. There the Writers' Union subsidised them, here they have to pay a fee to join. At home they know they have to praise, praise all the time, so the first thing they write is how high is the grass and how blue is the sky.' But such praise cuts no ice in Israel. Soon they are complaining instead, just like everyone else. At that moment, as we are about to sit down to lunch, Appelfeld's eldest son, Meir, returns on leave from the army. He is tall, much taller than his father, and dressed in khaki. This is unexceptional. Later, when I tell Philip Roth what he was carrying, he says, 'That's too good to be true. You wouldn't dare use it in a novel.' On one shoulder was a standard issue Uzi sub-machine gun; on the other, at the end of a rainbow-coloured strap, was a violin.

If only it were possible to clone Meir Appelfeld, to send

scores of athletic and aesthetic young men out into the world with their guns and violins and to say, 'Look, these are the new Jews, the Israelis, the luftmenshen of Sholem Aleichem and Marc Chagall earthed at last.' It would be wonderful, but it isn't possible, nor really desirable. It is hardly fair to tell a young man, You represent the best hope of our nation, even if it is true. Ask David Grossman.

15

DAVID GROSSMAN

Wednesday, 11 June 1986, the Institute of Jewish Affairs, London. 'You asked about myths, yes? The problem of Israel and of us sabras are those myths that were a very heavy burden upon ourselves to carry since the day we were born and even before. You know, I feel sometimes that life in Israel is never enough for the people, we have to relate to some ideal or some myth that we have to equal ourselves to, and we always lose because we cannot behave like mythological creatures. The myths are everywhere, take the myth of the sabra. All the literature about the myth of the sabra, even before Israel was established, described the sabra as a hero, as somebody who is very generous, very simple, very sincere. He was, of course, the antipode of the Jew from the diaspora and also his beloved son. And this myth really had a very strong and very heavy influence upon the young people who were born in Israel, because they had to stand for the principles that the myth had determined for them. What we got was generations of Israeli-born people who are very difficult to live with, not so sensitive, not so sophisticated. They consider themselves and their self-image as part of a big group, not as individuals. This is the most heavy burden of myth that we suffer from. And it influences every part of our life, because all the people that now take care of the business are sabras.

'You asked about the myths of Masada and Bar Kochba, yes? I must say that from the first time that I studied at school and I learned about Josephus Flavius I felt much more sympathy for him than for the other people that killed themselves, because I'm afraid of people that are capable of killing themselves, of people that see only two possibilities in life. Because they see the world as divided into only two possibilities they can be only victims or killers. And people like Flavius are the people who, when they will be in government, they will not kill, they will not become killers. Most of the people think that when they are dragged into a conflict they must be a killer or a victim, yes? When I wrote *The Smile of the Lamb* I felt like this.

'But in my new book *See Under 'Love'* I looked for other ways of not turning into a killer or a victim – you must determine what you are going to be, even if the situation looks lost. I will tell you a story. In this book there is a Jew, his name is Ginsberg. He is a madman. And he walks in the streets of Warsaw – before the war – and he stops people and he asks them, "Who am I? Who am I? Who am I?" All the time he keeps asking them, "Who am I?" And then the war came and people from the Gestapo came to Warsaw and he came to their headquarters where there was a Nazi investigator by the name of Orff. And Ginsberg came and he made Orff investigate him, because he heard in his upside-down way of thinking that the Gestapo people can take the truth out of a man, even though the man cannot reveal it to himself. And this Orff, he asked him, "Who are you?" and Ginsberg smiled because at last he knew he will have the truth taken out of him. And Orff kept asking him, "Who sent you?", "What is your mission here?", and he was happy at last to be answering all these substantial questions about humanity. Here you see how this Ginsberg managed to use the evil, to use it to a very deep and human goal. He uses the Nazi machine to take from him those torturing questions. For me it symbolises a way of not being a victim, because he's not a victim, this Ginsberg, because he controls the situation. But he's not a killer, he found another way of living.

'In Israel now there are people that really think that we have only two choices: either we will conquer or we will be conquered. They cannot accept the possibility of having another choice, another alternative. They are people who are so afraid of this other alternative they prefer war to a compromise. I really cannot understand it. They are exactly the people who would commit suicide in the case of Masada, yes? I will not do it, I will not kill my children and commit suicide, I think it's awful. I'm an atheist, of course. You know, on a programme about the relationship between secular and religious people I said in Hebrew, "I don't believe in God, I'm sorry but I don't believe in God, thank God." And I saw the faces of the cameraman, the director, and they looked quite bothered by the fact that they're not sure if they'll be allowed to broadcast it, because it will offend people to hear a Jew – and I'm a Jew, very much a Jew, I don't want anyone to hesitate about me being a Jew, because it's very important to me, I'm an Israeli, I'm a Jew, a non-religious Jew, and you can be a very very good Jew without believing in God. Judaism is not only religious of course. The religious people in Israel, they also take

176

from Judaism the things that they like, yes? So I can also take what I like from Judaism. Oh, it makes me mad, you know what they are doing? They are burning down the bus stops in Jerusalem!'

David Grossman, the speaker, is older than Meir Appelfeld, but six years younger than me. He has already fought in two wars and written four books. I have not read them, because they are written in Hebrew, but I am prepared to take his talent on trust, on the evidence of this single phrase: 'A salmon is a journey clothed in flesh.' It is 11 June 1986, an important date, the nineteenth anniversary of the end of the Six Day War. This means that as of tomorrow Israel will have been greater longer than it has been lesser by the difference of a day. And the next day two days and so on and so on until . . . or unless . . . Better an ellipsis than total eclipse. It seems to me that if Israel were to heed the voices of its writers – I hesitate to use the word 'prophets' – it need not see its light go out. I ask Grossman the following question, first formulated, you'll recall, in very different historical circumstances: 'As a result of the Viet Nam War Americans radically re-evaluated their own history. This, in turn, affected popular culture so that it became impossible to make a western with Indians as the baddies. More often than not it was the cavalry who were the villains. Has Lebanon had a similar effect within Israel?'

'Until now no novel has been published about the Lebanon War, but it's too close. I wrote a novel about Lebanon, but I didn't like it, it's awful because I wrote it when I came back from Lebanon. It was terrible to be there. I spent thirty-five days there and it was very difficult, it was a very concentrated thirty-five days and I had to do something with this, so I sat and wrote. But I know it's rubbish, it has no perspective, it has only anger – I will write something later. But a lot of poetry is written about

the Lebanese War. This I can understand; it's more concentrated, compressed. Like Ramy Ditzanny. I didn't meet him
but I like his poetry. He's very brutal and direct, maybe this is
the way to handle this war. No, I think the phenomenon of
rewriting our new history started before the Lebanon War, it
started after the '73 war, which was quite a trauma for us in
Israel. I was a soldier then, very young. And you cannot
imagine how awful it was, it aroused all the memories –
memories that I have never experienced myself, memories
from other days, from the Holocaust – because we really felt
that our very existence was in danger.

'It's very difficult being a writer in Israel, it's not like in the
USA where you can be detached from events, where you can
look from above and criticise everything because it doesn't have
a connection to your own life and to the life of your family. But
in Israel you have some commitment, you cannot say very
simple things about the situation because the situation is very
complicated, and writers who have a feel for the relativity of
things know that nothing is sure.

'But on the other hand I tell myself there are enough people
that will take care of the practical aspects and of the half-truths
and of the relative values, and that writers, people who create,
don't have to pay attention to the actual situation, they have to
determine values and atmosphere that will in the long run
influence the practical things in Israel.

'It is very difficult, really very difficult, but I can say now the
fact that I sat down and wrote *See Under 'Love'* about the
Holocaust – and I'm not a survivor, of course, also not the son
of survivors – is part of an attempt to deal with things that were
almost a taboo in Israel, yes? Since the end of the Six Day War
only one novel has been written about the Israeli occupation of
the West Bank, this is *The Smile of the Lamb*. I cannot

understand how authors avoid dealing with this problem – it's nineteen years, not one year, since the withdrawal from Lebanon. I wrote *See Under 'Love'* because I felt that what was written about the Holocaust was also a kind of myth that on one side made an idolisation and an idealisation of the Jews as victims, and on the other side it made a monsterisation of the Nazis, and I as a human being had no way of reaching those two monuments. What I did wasn't really rewriting history, it was rewriting the attitude to history. By writing I free myself from these taboos, and it's wonderful, because I see that the world, far from being an enemy, is constituted of materials that are all in me – really, everything that is in the world is in me, and it gives me a feeling of being at one with the world. For me writing is a kind of responsibility to bear, and it becomes more and more demanding from book to book, and it really frightens me because I know that in the next book I'll have to write about deeper things within me, and to be more sincere and brave and really give myself away.'

Having gone public for the first time in 1970 I understand Grossman's hesitant compulsion to be an exhibitionist; see, for evidence, the first chapter of *Blood Libels*, which concludes with my alter ego, Jake Silkstone, entering Sunnyhill Park, Hendon, wearing nothing but a raincoat and sandals and scandalising 'a new generation of philippina-eyed housegirls with a sight of the real me'. Like Grossman, Jake Silkstone also has a sense of terrestrial wholeness, but in his case (and I use this in the medicinal sense) it is a shared fever, a genocidal madness. I blame it on life in the diaspora, that third-rate drama.

PART FOUR

THE

THIN

GREEN

LINE

1

SACRED COWS

At a recent conference entitled 'Intellectual Freedom in the Jewish Community' Steven Zipperstein, lecturer in modern Jewish history at Oxford University, made the following statement: 'Can it really be doubted that intellectual freedom exists? The British Jewish community boasts a writer – also the literary editor of the *Jewish Chronicle* – whose most recent novel features a Hendon rabbi engaging in unspeakable acts that would shock and titillate the most blasé and sophisticated. A prominent female liberal rabbi announces publicly her penchant for foods considered forbidden by Jews since their ancient wanderings in Middle Eastern deserts and my Monday *Guardian* prints a sequel in her continuing ruminations on AIDS. . . . How much more freedom do the organisers of this symposium feel intellectuals should exercise? What more have Clive Sinclair and Rabbi Julia Neuberger to reveal?'

I recognise that Steven Zipperstein's remarks are merely an amusing preamble to a more serious oration – the conference was arranged by the *Jewish Quarterly* and occasioned by the forced resignation of that journal's previous editor who, it was deemed, could not serve both an official organisation, the Institute of Jewish Affairs, and publish neo-Bundist and other renegade articles in an independent magazine, lest the latter be mistaken for the views of the former, so he was given a choice, which was really no choice since only one job offered a salary, the IJA or the *JQ* – and would merely wish to add that ignorance of my views rather than respect for them is what protects me from the elders of Zion.

I am convinced that this review from the *Jewish Gazette* is a true expression of the *vox populi*, were there more readers among that far from silent majority. 'Knowing Clive Sinclair's reputation as a literary editor and author, I approached the task of reviewing his latest book, *Blood Libels*, with eager antici- pation. I was in for a shock! . . . Perhaps what I found most distasteful was the fact that Clive Sinclair chose such subjects as a rabbi, Israeli Embassy staff and an Israeli woman for the vehicles of his sexual fantasy. Add to that a thinly disguised attack on the establishment, particularly the newspaper *Jewish Voice*, which appeared to differ in name only from the real thing, strong views on the Lebanon campaign, and a dangerous combination of fact and fiction – enough to make the reader start to think the fiction might also be true – and it added up to a book that was definitely not for me. In fact it left me wondering if some of the time spent writing it would not have been better spent on the psycho-analyst's couch, trying to discover the reasons for his apparent obsessions with the bodily functions and sex.' This from a woman who would doubtless scream blue murder if the Soviets locked a refusnik in the loony bin for daring to express his views. I might also ask why my treatment of rabbis and Israelis left such a bad taste. Would it be all right with her if only goyim got shot or raped? Here, surely, is one of those English Jews for whom Zionism is a substitute religion, the golden calf become sacred cow. Israel right or wrong. What are the heresies these zealots abhor? If Zionism is to retain its moral strength it must be able to answer them back.

2

FIL-KHARIJ

It is question time at London's Institute of Contemporary Arts. Edward Said is back once more; this time in conversation with the novelist Salman Rushdie, the subject being the exiled professor's new book *After the Last Sky*, subtitled *Palestinian Lives*, which, as it happens, I read while travelling in Israel. The seminar room is packed. Video cameras are recording the event for the benefit of our descendants. Accordingly a boom microphone hovers above the audience, moving from talking head to talking head. Its shadow falls on the wall just behind Said's own cranium. To me it looks like an auctioneer's gavel about to sell the disputed land to the most deserving bidder. Others might see it as threatening, like the ice pick that did for Trotsky.

This, I suspect, would be the majority view; for death threats are valued highly at the ICA. Edward Said has had one, we were told, from the Jewish Defense League, which is a bit like saying he gets hot salt beef on rye from Blooms. What else does he expect from such people, a Valentine? Having established that the long arm of Jewish vengeance can make life as dangerous for a Palestinian in New York as it is in Jerusalem or Hebron, Rushdie and Said, a formidable double act, are quick to separate anti-Zionism from antisemitism.

'Criticising Zionism is like playing chess against a grand-master,' said Said, meaning that the Holocaust gambit is unbeatable. I know Salman, have met Said once before, and would happily swear to the fact that both are Judeophiles.

185

Though when people say that they like Jews but aren't so crazy on Israelis I cannot help but think of Sholom Aleichem's satire 'On America', in which an immigrant assures the folks back home that Yankees love Jews but hate their beards, which they cut off in the streets.

Nor am I as convinced as Rushdie and Said that anti-Zionism and antisemitism are such distinct entities. Were the men who locked themselves into Istanbul's Neve Shalom synagogue in the summer of 1986 and massacred the congregation anti-Zionists or antisemites? Doubtless some, such as those who peddle the libel that the Holocaust was a Nazi-Zionist collaboration or, more specifically, Mohammed Yamani, author of *The Beersheba Triangle* – in which Israelis, disguised as Arab terrorists, machine-gun Jewish children merely to blacken the name of Palestine – will say that this too is a Jewish plot to swing the world's sympathy (a slander Said scrupulously eschews).

Which is not – and now it's my turn to offer a disclaimer – to endorse the ugly words of Ariel Sharon who quickly defined 'the terrible pogrom against Jews during their prayers in the synagogue in Istanbul' as 'the terrible and exclusive reply by the Palestinians and their supporters . . . to Israel's pleadings for peace and her readiness for concessions'.

Just as I distance myself from the Jewish Defense League, and would expect Said to acknowledge the difference between us, so Said should not be dismissed as Shelley did Castlereagh after the Peterloo Massacre: 'I met Murder on the way – / He had a mask like Castlereagh – / Very smooth he looked, yet grim; / Seven blood-hounds followed him.'

Notwithstanding his half-hearted exchange with Amos Oz, recorded earlier, his case – made in print and in person – must be considered publicly, lest we – I mean the Jews – develop the hypocritical paranoia of people with something to hide. It may be that in the end we will have to echo the words one of Said's relatives had printed on a card: 'Your story is very moving. Thank you very much. But I cannot contribute.' But not before we have heard it.

That we, the Jews, have a story is undeniable, though, it must be admitted, Said has his doubts. He would contest its relationship to Palestine by rejecting the idea of a redemptive homeland, for Jews or for his own people. The story he would ascribe to the Palestinians is essentially modern, but as yet lacks a definitive version – a grave deficiency. Moreover, when the story of the Palestinians is recited it is usually based upon the Jewish model of exile and return. It is a parallel Said hotly disputes, rejecting such words as 'exodus', 'diaspora' and 'ghetto' and replacing them with their Arabic equivalents. In *After the Last Sky* he offers the following argument: 'I do not like to call it a Palestinian *diaspora*: there is only an apparent symmetry between our exile and theirs. Besides, the diaspora no longer exists spiritually and culturally as it once did in Central Europe, with tragic figures like Kafka, Schoenberg, and Benjamin at its core. . . . In any event our *ghurba* or *manfa* is a much different thing because, most simply, our demographic ties to Palestine today are more substantial than Judaism's in the period before 1948. . . . The biggest concentration of Palestinians, then, is in the Arab world, unlike diaspora Zionism, which was largely a European phenomenon.'

'The absolute essence of the matter,' says Said to a questioner at the ICA, 'is that the Jewish problem was exported to Palestine.' I should like to tell Professor Said a little story. Most Jews, according to the old joke, have two synagogues, one to go to, one to shun; my friend Yosl Bergner has two cobblers, an Argentinian, already introduced, and a Pole. In fact Yosl once

187

painted a sign for the latter: two shoes floating in the blue sky. That's how it was in the diaspora: two shoes but no ground. It hung outside the ex-Pole's workshop until Yosl became a famous artist and the cobbler decided that his sign was too valuable to leave in the street. 'Now,' says Yosl, 'he advertises his trade with a shoe and a glass of water. The glass is really from Poland, where it was supposed to protect against lightning and other forms of bad luck.' Much good it did anyone in the old country. 'It's not easy living in Israel,' another friend tells me, 'it's not like living in London, New York or California. It's not easy living here among three million Jews with the economy and the climate. It makes a lot of people wonder why we are here, and a lot of my contemporaries have forgotten the answer.' The answer, of course, is those two airborne shoes. Here at last is terra firma. To which Said would probably answer, 'But you are stepping on someone else's toes.' 'So make a little room.' What else can we say?

The Palestinians' *manfa*, their exile, is specific, the result of the *nakba*, the disaster of 1948, whereas our *diaspora* is so far removed from its historical cause as to be mythic. A major value of myth, however, is that it preserves memory through ritual re-enactment; for instance the words 'Next year in Jerusalem' that are said every Pesach whether in Cracow or Addis Ababa. Without their potency who knows how long the memory of Palestine will remain with the Said family? 'How does a Palestinian father tell his son and daughter,' writes Said, 'that Lebanon (Egypt, Syria, Jordan, New York) is where we are, but not where we are *from*? How does a mother confirm her intimate recollections of childhood in Palestine to her children, now that the facts, the places, even the names are no longer allowed to exist?' Collective memory, lacking an institution-alised history, is subject to human frailty, the worst of which is forgetting. But once a history becomes institutionalised it inevitably becomes fictionalised in the passage from generation to generation. It is all very well for Said to suggest that the Palestinian experience, being contemporary, is more valid, but unless it becomes verbalised, in the manner of our story, it will quickly become meaningless.

It seems to me, and I could be wrong, for I am talking of nuances, that Said recognises this in his heart. At the ICA he described his desire to return to Palestine as a metaphorical concept, which I took to mean that he is prepared to bequeath to his children a homeland constructed out of language which, if the world is generous, will have a correspondence in reality, and will be there for them all if New York should pall. What Said seems to require of us now may be deduced from this quote, which a fellow academic addressed to an Israeli colleague on neutral territory: 'I'm from Haifa. Don't worry, I don't want my house back. What I want from you is a sign that you did wrong.' And then what? Supposing the Israelis say, 'Sorry we trod on your feet,' which would not be such a hard thing, after all? Would Said then concede that events occurring before 1890, though no longer part of living memory, have some bearing on the case, and that Jews have spiritual as well as political rights in the Levant? Would he wonder what that tragic figure, Franz Kafka, who did not live to see the Holocaust, saw in Zionism?

It may sound odd but Edward Said reminds me of Isaac Bashevis Singer; both, after all, write lovingly about the villages of their youth from the vantage of Manhattan. Said, like Singer, became a willing exile, anxious to make his way in a world that was, through the enticements of modernism, already destabilising the traditional village or shtetl values. There is

189

therefore in *After the Last Sky*, as there is in all Singer's books, a measure of guilt. This shows itself in Said's attitude to the Palestinians who stayed to become Israeli citizens, those who are *min al dakhil*, from the interior. Once they were different 'in a pejorative sense', contaminated. Now they are still different, 'but privileged'. Said, on the other hand (or shore), lives *fil-kharij*, in the exterior. These phrases give off a psychological resonance, implying that it is somehow less alienating to be *min al dakhil* than *fil-kharij*, closer to what may be called real life.

It was this feeling, certainly, that impelled Kafka to learn Hebrew in anticipation of his journey into the interior, a trip that was aborted by his own insides. What stops Said? The absence of Palestine? Of course. But also the snares of Babylon. Instead the professor writes a book like *After the Last Sky*, intellectually provoking and emotionally evocative, but no substitute for being there.

As I said, I read it *min al dakhil*, in my own heartland. Did it make me feel guilty? Not really, for I was in that Israel which would embrace the Palestinians, given half a chance. Did I feel like a trespasser among trespassers? No. So I have nothing to contribute to the proceedings? On the contrary, if it were in my power I'd admit that Israel had grown a bit too big for its boots and give the Palestinians a state on the West Bank. But it isn't. This is not something that can be solved *fil-kharij*, even in the Institute of Contemporary Arts, but only *min al dakhil*, in Israel. But solved it must be. And soon.

3

MIN AL DAKHIL

Anton Shammas, the author of *Arabesque*, lives *min al dakhil*, and writes in the language of the interior. This is his justification. 'Exile for the Palestinians is the language of confusion,' he has said. 'There's no grace in being a confused refugee. The Arabs of Israel, me included, live in a state of confusion inside the state of Israel. For me, only the language of grace, meaning Hebrew, could gracefully utter my confusion. Speaking of confusion – I belong to the Arab minority living within the Jewish minority, living within the Arab majority in the Middle East. Babushka-style: once you unfold a layer of confusion you find out that there is another layer within that layer down to the bitter end. It's a rather crowded Babushka, and sometimes it's quite impossible to point out who is our ventriloquist; is it our homeland or rather our exile? The only certain thing is that we are the dummies of both.' Except that Shammas is far from dumb.

Edward Said, though properly respectful of those who have chosen to dwell *min al dakhil*, is anxious to preserve Arabic against the encroachments of Hebrew. 'The standard Hebrew method for transliterating Arabic words and names,' he writes in *After the Last Sky*, 'has now completely taken over the American press; this enrages me to an absurd degree.' What, I wonder, would Said make of *Arabesque*, in which the Arabs converse, not in their mother tongue, but in Shammas's eloquent Hebrew? The comparison may seem strange, but I am put in mind of the assimilated Jews in Aharon Appelfeld's

191

novels who now speak Hebrew instead of their native German. The fact that two such different writers can translate their feelings so successfully into the language of the interior is surely Israel's greatest and most secure achievement. We may be what we eat, but we are also what we think, and language more than anything helps define what we think we are.

I am anxious to meet such a linguistic prodigy as Shammas, but he is not so keen. Fortunately Jonathan's partner at Scopus Films, Uri Shin'ar, wants to make a documentary about Shammas and thinks that I may be able to help. We discuss the project over a beer at the Writers' House. 'I envy Uri,' said Jonathan, by way of description, 'he knows the difference between right and wrong.' He certainly knows what he wants to do in the film. Shammas was born in 1950, in a Christian village near the Lebanese border called Fassuta. Some of his family still live there. It provides the setting for *Arabesque*. That is, therefore, where the film will begin. Shammas's parents, however, moved to Haifa when the lad was twelve. Here he received his formal education, at an Arab-Jewish school. Today Shammas's plays are performed at one of Haifa's theatres, where the cast is equally mixed. The camera will follow him as he puts the actors through their paces. Jerusalem will be the third strand in the film, as it is in Shammas's life. He has an apartment in Jerusalem, in the quiet Jewish suburb of Rehavia, an odd address for such a committed intellectual. All this Uri tells me. Can I be of assistance? There doesn't seem much left for me to do. Perhaps if I could compare my right to live in Israel, under the Law of Return, with that of Shammas, who has at least squatter's rights if not a birthright? 'How?' asks Uri. 'Well,' I say, 'we'll present Shammas's views first.'

These are well known in Israel, the literary success of *Arabesque* having had political consequences, not the sort you'd expect, the chief of them being a public row between Shammas and Haifa's best-known citizen, A. B. Yehoshua, a leftist writer whose previous works were translated into Arabic by Shammas himself. This is not some literary slanging match, but an argument about fundamentals. In an essay entitled 'Kitsch 22' (wherein Milan Kundera, of all people, is accused of being a little kitsch, a little too eager to please the patrons of the Jerusalem Book Fair, by calling Israel 'the true heart of Europe, a strange heart which lies far from the body'), Shammas explains what it means to be an Arab in Israel. 'The position, which we may call "Kitsch 22", can be described as follows: the state of Israel defines itself as a Jewish state (or even "the state of the Jews") and demands of its Arab citizens to fulfil their citizenship, but when they do so, it promptly informs them that their participation in the state is merely social, and that for the political fulfilment of their identity they must look elsewhere (i.e. to the Palestinian nation); when they do so, and look elsewhere for their national identity, the state at once charges them with subversion, and, needless to say, as subversives they cannot be accepted as Israelis – and so on, in circles, ad infinitum.' Shammas's solution is not a Palestinian state, as such, but simply the dejudification of Israel.

4

THE LAW OF RETURN

In his column for *Ha'ir*, a Tel Aviv weekly, Shammas set about the Law of Return, racist legislation in his opinion. But he didn't argue for its immediate repeal, his satirical approach being more subtle and more painful. Israel, he wrote, should 'announce during its Jubilee celebrations in 1998 – hopefully assuming that, by then, the Jewish-Arab conflict will be settled – that world Jewry will be given ten years more to "make aliya" and that the gates of aliya and automatic citizenship will close in 2008.' A. B. Yehoshua wasn't amused. The Law of Return, he insisted, was 'the moral basis of Zionism'. Like Amos Oz he assumed that any eventual Palestinian state would enact its own Law of Return, which would allow Edward Said, for example, the option of being either Palestinian or American. Yehoshua being in no doubt what a good Palestinian should choose. Thus he told Shammas, 'If you want to live in a country having an independent Palestinian character, arise, take your portable belongings, and move 100 metres eastward to the independent Palestinian state that will be situated next to Israel.' Likewise, when he addressed a group of French Jews he called them 'Frenchmen with a thin coating of Jewishness', and informed them that if they wanted to be fully Jewish they should move to Israel. So who is the racist: A. B. Yehoshua, who believes in Israel for Jews and Palestine for Arabs; or a settler who is happy to live among Arabs providing the place is not called Palestine; or Edward Said, whose nationalistic views seem to mirror those of Yehoshua?

I put Anton Shammas's suggestion to Uri Avnery when we met in London. It appealed, the Law of Return being 'the only thing I have to answer that I am both for and against it'. He is ambivalent, in other words. 'I cannot like a law which makes an official distinction between people according to race, religion, colour of skin or whatever,' he continued. 'One unfortunate result has been that since then Israel is ravaged by the question "Who is a Jew?" And this will go on forever. More governments have fallen on this question in Israel than on any serious problem. If you are interested in this I can add a small detail which perhaps you don't know. At the time when Ben Gurion promulgated this law the Attorney General – in Israel it's called the legal advisor to the government – was Yakov Shimshon Shapira, one of the most important jurists in Israel. And he told me in private once that he advised Ben Gurion not to enact this law – and he's a rabid Zionist – not to enact the law because he foresaw all these problems. You don't need a law, he said. Every government decides who it lets in and who it does not let in, so if the majority in Israel wants to let all the Jews in it can do it. Therefore the law was superfluous from the beginning. On the other hand, I understand why the law was promulgated: it was a symbolic act to express the central mission of the state, as the majority of its inhabitants at that time saw it and still see it; namely to be a refuge to Jews who are persecuted and who want to come to join the nation. And once the law is there, to abolish it would become another symbolic act, saying we want to close the state to those Jews. And I wouldn't agree to that either.

'I am the chairman of a party which is Jewish-Arab, in which the Arab element is very important. I have great trouble to explain this to Arab colleagues, even in my own party. I tell them that it has become a kind of paper statue, which has no real importance at all; it's purely symbolic, both in the positive and the negative sense. It's purely symbolic because the Jews don't come. We have got a negative aliya.'

The controversy spills over into the Writers' House, when I am having lunch with Shulamit Lapid, Tommy Lapid and Moshe Dor. 'There is a great debate among authors,' says Shulamit, 'a very strong debate among the left wing, within the family, as it were.' According to her it began when A. B. Yehoshua demanded of Anton Shammas: why do you never condemn Palestinian atrocities as we shout about Jewish ones? Sides have been taken, between those who agree and those who are, according to Tommy, 'self-loathing Palestinian lovers'. This leads to a real argument between Tommy and Moshe, though it is difficult to tell if hostility is masked by banter or if they are friends who enjoy a spat. Finally Moshe calls Tommy the devil incarnate, a wolf in the clothes of a lamb.

Shammas, equally forthright, accused Yehoshua of wanting to complete the Palestinian exodus – to him Yehoshua must have sounded like a Polish antisemite who, having complained about the *Ostjuden*, is even more suspicious of their enlightened co-religionists, his neighbours. But this, I think, is a misinterpretation. Yehoshua is a humane, sophisticated man; to him a homeland is not essentially a place of residence, but a society in which like-minded people can determine their joint destiny; he is, in another word, a nationalist. It all depends, therefore, upon how you define those like-minded citizens; a racist would cite genes or blood or maybe colour; a nationalist would talk in terms of shared cultural values, of a guiding text, be it a constitution or a popular myth, if the Bible may be so called. In any case place of birth is of no great significance.

I was born, as a matter of fact, at the Old Court nursing home in Ealing, a now demolished landmark on my former route to London Airport, on 19 February 1948, three months before

196

David Ben Gurion, a dead ringer for my father, proclaimed Israel's statehood at a hall in Tel Aviv. The nursing home was picked on account of its proximity to the attic in which I was conceived, though I like to think it was because my parents had half a mind to light out for Palestine instead of stepping up the social ladder that would take them, eventually, to Hendon. As I have explained, it took me nineteen years to complete the journey begun by my birth, a journey I have been repeating on a more or less annual basis ever since, my own Law of Return. Does my Jewishness give me the right to invoke the real thing, should I ever decide to make aliya? Indeed, of what does it consist?

Here is another shoe story from Yosl's studio. It is late August 1986 and I am, as in 1978, looking for a picture to put on a book jacket. That done, a visitor shows up, another artist. It turns out that his father was also a local cobbler, having once had a kiosk on wheels. 'There is a whole correspondence – almost voluminous enough to be literature – about how my father tried to have his wheels removed and a permanent site established,' says Yosl's guest. This was in the days of the British when the Wandering Jew was still considered an admirable role model. There was a riding school nearby and, as compensation, the cobbler was given the drinks concession on race days. His customers, it seems, all wore long shiny boots which fascinated the cobbler's son, so much so that he stole one and sanded it to see if the shine went all the way through. What did A. B. Yehoshua call French Jews? Well, I wonder if I am not like that boot, an Englishman with a thin coating of Jewishness. Though I am not very English either.

Recently I walked down the King's Road in Chelsea with two Israelis: Aharon Appelfeld and his younger son, Yitzhak. Yitzhak, as it happens, was born in Oxford and spent his first

197

weeks in that city. As a treat before conscription Aharon has taken off a summer to show him around Oxford and London. We were looking for an art supplier to get some pens and paper for Aharon's eldest son, Meir, an artist as well as a violinist and soldier. The emporium we found was full of the rudiments of art, and run by women from the English upper classes. It was near closing and the owner, a masculine type with a cravat, said to us, her last customers, 'Come on, boys, it's time to go.' Aharon was wearing a dark jacket and a black peaked cap. He paid for his purchases and the woman, noticing his thick accent, said to him, 'Are you from Russia or *somewhere*?' 'Israel,' he replied. Not expecting to have *somewhere* so precisely defined the woman and her assistants giggled. Yes, Israel is somewhere, terra firma for Aharon and Yitzhak, but what about me? I am not from Russia or somewhere, though my grandparents were, but I am not from England either – the woman was as foreign to me as she was to Aharon.

Aharon and Yitzhak at St Albans. It emerged that they were kosher, so I sought out a suitably slaughtered fowl in Hendon and prepared it with juice, peppers and apricots in the Israeli fashion. During the meal Aharon described his brief spell as a dancing instructor at Netanya. It was, he said, while he was teaching salon dancing, the tango and the like, that he first became aware of the frailty of the human frame. His pupils were in their forties, survivors from Europe; the women plumpish, no longer supple, the men in red ties which looked ungainly over their paunches. He remembered how their faces flushed and spots of sweat appeared on their foreheads, he recalled the details long enough to incorporate them into his heart-breaking allegory, *Badenheim 1939*. He spoke as he writes, quietly. He has no need to raise his voice. His words

198

have been authenticated by misfortune.

After dinner we played chess. 'A Jewish game,' said Aharon, and no less revealing than dancing. I look at the pieces in much the same way as the Israeli typesetters looked at the English characters; I know the moves, but not the language that will make sense of them. Aharon's father and grandfather were both great players. They would shout or even sing while they trounced their opponents, 'Call yourself a chess player? You are no good!' Their descendant was much kinder: as I faced defeat he merely mentioned, *en passant*, what his grandfather would have said – 'You need a miracle.' Chess is indeed a Jewish game, as Edward Said also observed, and I am no good at it; I am responsive, without strategies or structures, or any scholarly inheritance to draw upon.

As Irving Howe said of Philip Roth, I seem to be cut off from any Jewish tradition. You only have to compare me with Anatoly Sharansky, formerly assimilated, who also became a committed Zionist in that year of miracles, 1967. What did he do in the penal colony, his home from home, to retain his sanity? 'I played lots of chess. I can play chess without a board, without looking at a board, and I did it frequently in the punishment cells.' There speaks a real Jew. When he comes to London for the first time in September 1986, five thousand flock to hear him – now I know how many yarmulkas it takes to fill the Albert Hall – the Chief Rabbi and the Israeli Ambassador among them. Sharansky appears on stage and we all rise, as if the scrolls had just been brought out of the ark on Rosh Hashana. His speech done, he leads us in a community singsong: the Hatikva, Israel's national anthem. Here is the Law of Return's vindication!

But how can I persuade Anton Shammas that lousy chess players should be let in too? How can I, a tourist on a brief visit from St Albans, say to that resident of Jerusalem, whose problems of identity make mine seem like a luxury item, this is more my country than yours? Get out of that one, Houdini!

'Can you?' asks Uri Shin'ar.

5

THE VILLAGE AND THE SUBURB

When Shammas speaks of a 'New Israeliness' he is, I think, being pragmatic, creating a nation out of those who were born there, himself included, which would explain his reluctance to move to a state of Palestine, should there ever be one on the West Bank. This, it seems to me, is essentially the outlook of a villager, of someone who has the seasonal rhythms of Fassuta buried in his being. Except that Shammas no longer lives in Fassuta; he has joined the outside world, as irrevocably as Singer or Said, and he could just as easily be in Amman or Damascus (not to mention New York) as Jerusalem. No necessity binds him to the latter, which is not to question his right to be there. Nothing binds me to Hendon, except the presence of my parents. Suburbanites, unlike villagers, do not expect their offspring to remain in the family house. On the contrary, we are expected to break surface and conquer the city itself. Once my father was a furniture manufacturer of some repute. Before my approaching barmitzvah made attendance at the local synagogue a necessity we went to his factory every

Saturday morning. He enjoyed showing me off to his workers, and the smell of wood chips and varnish still sets off memories of Proustian dimensions, but there was never a hint of 'One day, son, all this will be yours.' God forbid! I was expected to go on to better things: the professions. The village is a natural habitat. The suburb is full of motels disguised as homes. The disguise serves two purposes: (a) to establish the illusion of permanence: (b) to facilitate a quick escape. Even in England there is the abiding fear that one day the facade will crack and that death in its black-shirt will come storming through. Outward stability is merely the symptom of this internal insecurity. Upward mobility is the only escape. So here I am, pushed out into the world by my proud parents, still looking for a place of my own, and lacking a Fassuta whither I may return. In short, suburbs are meant to be left, to be vacated for the next generation of immigrants. Unlike villages. It was, therefore, a much bigger thing for the family Shammas to quit Fassuta than it was for me to leave Hendon; it was, in a manner of speaking, unnatural. Anton Shammas has entered a new society, attracted not by its bucolic charms but by its intellectual stimulations. Uri Avnery, a sympathetic observer, believes that the Palestinians, as exemplified by Shammas, are becoming more Jewish than the Israeli Jews. Anyway, it is a society that owes very little to Fassuta, though that may yet change, but much to the history that brought my grandparents to White-chapel and my parents to Hendon. With the suburb behind me and eternity ahead, Israel is an immensely attractive place to stay awhile. The more so since I am a writer and stories seem to be one of its national industries.

It occurs to me that as my interest in Israel has increased so has my concern for narrative fiction. My first novel, *Bibliosexuality*, was picaresque, to say the least. It ended with my

201

hero and his lover disappearing, a logical consequence of the parthenogenetic form, which can only be terminated arbitrarily. The more I wrote the more dissatisfied I became with this accidental structure. What I sought were inevitable conclusions, not superimposed by propaganda or dogma, but by the story itself. Indeed, by a nice twist, it was a strong story, 'Uncle Vlad', which led me indirectly to half the characters who people this book. Edward Said, on the other hand, concedes in the Introduction to *After the Last Sky* that his book will not tell a consecutive story 'since the main features of our present existence are dispossession, dispersion', and that the style will therefore be 'unconventional, hybrid and fragmentary'. I am not going to pretend that modernism and postmodernism are unknown in Israel or foreign to me. I merely wish to draw attention to the importance of narrative, both in fiction and to nations.

What Shammas's 'New Israeliness' lacks is a story that links land and people: Jewish history, in other words. Edward Said, for one, accepts the importance of history, if not myth, and encourages his people to record their experiences as the Jews have done, so that they may, in Heine's phrase, carry their homeland on their backs. History enriches a language as blood fertilises the soil. A fact acknowledged by the Soviets. 'They cannot put the Hebrew language on trial,' said one of their victims in a memorable speech. 'They cannot put verbs and nouns in prison. So they arrest Iosif Begun.' For giving Hebrew lessons.

'Can language substitute for a homeland?' asked Shammas in a recent essay, in which he told the story of an Arab friend who took up a teaching post at Berkeley. 'Ten years ago, before he left for the States, he was frantically looking for a wife, so they could share the agony of self-exile. I asked him once if it wouldn't be wiser to find himself a green-carded American. He said, "I'm looking for a woman that when I put my weary head against her arm I want to hear her blood murmuring in Arabic." He did eventually find one, and they have been happily hearing each other's blood ever after. Uri Zvi Greenberg once described Hebrew as being his blood-tongue, failing to be his mother-tongue. The people who were banished from their home by Uri Zvi Greenberg found it hard, if not utterly impossible, to make do with language, evasive and ephemeral as it is. One might wonder, can language be a substitute for the scent of orange orchards smelt by a fleeing Palestinian in '48?' No. Such language could never be anything more than an anaemic shadow, since it refers to the blossom rather than the root. It is, in short, the sort of romantic prose that served Monyeh Bergner so badly in his attempt to colonise the promised land; and it leads to an overblown version of history that is impossible to maintain in the face of reality. Orange trees, as far as I am aware, smell much the same in Jaffa as in Sidon. Shammas knows better than to depend upon such sugary stuff for sustenance. He has the language – Hebrew – and the land – Israel – and he is saying, 'That's enough.' He doesn't require any history to justify his presence; all he need do is to point to Fassuta. He is a modern, self-made man, but he has roots, though they do not necessarily nourish his present pose. The game he is playing is bold indeed. He has entered a strange society, which itself has overwhelmed the local culture, and said, in effect, 'We're all in the same boat now. Let go of your pasts as I have left Fassuta and let us live together in the New Jerusalem.' This would certainly lead to a normal life, if adopted by all, but it would also erase the state's universal pretensions. Whether it would be worth the price is not for an outsider to judge. Such self-confidence exposes the distance between Shammas and Said – for the latter, in order to sustain his Palestinian identity, must establish the very history Shammas seems prepared to jettison, which itself will grow out of Arabic, Shammas's second language. The question is whether the Palestinian cause will survive the interim.

Israel somehow lasted for two thousand years without a land. It was an innocent time, whose passing some regret, notwithstanding the fate of those who kept the dream of a return alive. George Steiner – like my dolphins – maintains that a Jew's 'true homeland is a text and an almost unfathomable body of law and ethical argument; not a nation state'. A statement somewhat strained by the existence of Israel. What Israel has done is to return that text to reality and, what is more, create new texts in the language of the original. The result may lack the atmosphere of a university, Steiner's Utopia, but it offers a more realistic refuge than a text, however holy. This, then, is my justification: I am Jewish because of my history, because I want to remain part of a story which starts *Bereshis boro elohim*, only I see 'In the beginning God created . . .' History opens the door, then language shuts it in my face. Therein lies Shammas's advantage over me: his command of the language of the interior – my interior. He has, as it were, called my bluff, as Ben Gurion called Steiner's. Steiner can complain that Israel has produced no Einsteins, but what can I do? Look for flaws in Shammas's knowledge to expose him as a parvenu, as Gore Vidal did to Norman Podhoretz? God forbid! Or learn Hebrew and write a better novel than *Arabesque*?

'What's the answer?' asks Uri. 'I'm not sure,' I reply, 'logically it should be yes, but I cannot see it happening.' Uri, no dabbler in uncertainties, loses interest. 'Don't call us,' he says, 'we'll call you.' Instead I call Anton Shammas and, by dropping Uri's name, get an invitation.

His apartment displays the utilitarian neatness of a good lecturer's office, rather than the quotidian messiness of a place that is lived in. Does this mean that he feels like a guest in his own home, or is it a sign of dedication to his craft? Both, I assume. So I feel guilty as a writer on account of the work that obviously gets done here, and uneasy as a Jew because he doesn't seem comfortable in God's own country. I therefore address him with the exaggerated politeness of an overanxious host who wants his strange guest to know he is more than welcome. Meanwhile, he offers me a beer which I, in my clumsiness, spill on his hitherto spotless rug. We talk. Or rather I listen to this Israeli who quotes Bialik, writes novels in Hebrew, lives in West Jerusalem, and who isn't Jewish. Or is he? Can his 'New Israeliness' really exclude Judaism? Or does he anticipate a new synthetic race of Habs and Hab-nots? Shammas tells, in 'Kitsch 22', how he once shared a room with a piano. The European instrument in the Arab environment disturbed him so much that he was unable to sleep until, after many nights, he tried to play the thing. He was subsequently instructed in basic technique by bona fide musicians; the left hand, he learned, provided the background while the right developed the theme. 'How are the Arabs in Israel to play their culture with the right hand, when the left hand of the Jewish majority sets the framework chords?' asks Shammas. His answer is to use both hands, 'to write an Arab story in Hebrew letters'. That's the crescendo, the climax is dedicated to A. B. Yehoshua, who 'does not realise that his left hand is already part of my Israeli being, just as at least one finger of his right hand is one of mine'.

There is also a saying: the right hand does not know what the left is doing (and vice versa). I have tried to learn a bit about the Palestinians, but I would never presume to understand them.

How could I? I don't begin to understand myself, let alone the Jews, which leads to the following basic question (I borrow the form from Edward Said): 'How does a Jewish father tell his son that St Albans is where we are, but not where we are from?'

6

THE SHIP OF FOOLS

What, to be precise, do I tell Seth, my five-year-old son, as we board the Green Line bus at the start of his first visit to Israel, land of the Jews? He knows he is Jewish, but has no idea what that means. If anything he thinks of himself as an American – having been born in Santa Cruz, California – and likes to pretend that he is the resident expert on the American way of life, specialising in cowboys and Indians.

'Once upon a time,' I began, 'just after the Creation, before the world was properly settled, when the earth was still fiery and the oceans bubbled, people lived in boats instead of countries. This is the story of one boat, the Good Ship Israel, and the people who sailed upon her, the Jews. Well, for many years everything was plain sailing, too plain, for the passengers grew bored and argued among themselves. A few, less foolish, warned them of their folly. These men were known as prophets, though they were more often called jokers. In exasperation the prophets cried, each in their turn, "This is a ship of fools!" And they were right. The Jews were so busy fighting one another that they failed to notice the pirates, whose flag was the wolf. These pirates were called Romans and their ambition was to capture every ship upon the sea. In this they nearly succeeded, taking vessels as distant as the Good Ship England.

'After they had captured the Good Ship Israel, which was not very difficult, they left their own captain in charge and went off after other prizes. The new captain was cruel, upon this everyone was agreed. "If you are of one mind," said the prophets, "you will be able to do anything." So the Jews stopped arguing, joined together and chucked the wicked captain into the sea. This made the Romans extremely angry. They counted the number of hairs in the drowned man's beard and killed the same number of Jews. The second captain they left behind was even worse than the first. "We shouldn't have listened to you," the people said to the prophets, "now we're in a bigger mess!" But at length the prophets prevailed and the Jews, united, tossed the second captain to the sharks. When the Romans returned they were determined to leave no Jew alive on the Good Ship Israel. In this, too, they nearly succeeded. Many were slaughtered, and those that survived were cursed, for the Romans spread the word that the Jews were bewitched and would bring bad luck to all who helped them. So the few remaining Jews stowed away on other ships, secretly, in ones and twos, like thieves in the night, praying that they would not be spotted.

'Among them,' I said to Seth, 'was your ancestor.' 'What's an ancestor?' he asked. 'A great-grandfather,' I replied.

'Many years passed, but separated, lonely and scared as they were, no Jew ever forgot that they once lived on their own ship. The Romans, considering even this a challenge, changed the boat's name and gave it to new sailors. Now all that remained to the Jews was an old name and a secret language only they understood. But even this was too much for their enemies.

'One day a new leader arose among those who hated the Jews and he was wickeder than the worst pirate chief. "If it weren't for the Jews," he screamed, "no boat would ever sink. Our boat is sinking. My people, you know the cause! If we want to save our ship of state we must kill the Jews. All of them. Even the babies." So his people turned upon the Jews and slaughtered all they could find – even the babies – until the sea was red with blood. Nor was the massacre confined to one boat. The madness spread and soon everyone was killing the evil-eyed secret-tongued Jews. A few escaped in life boats. But where could they go? Then they remembered the stories their parents had told them of the Good Ship Israel. It was these stories that saved them. . . .' The rest is history. 'Did they make it?' asks Seth. 'You'll see,' I reply.

I like the fact that we are on a Green Line bus, for, as you know, the Green Line means something in Israel too, being the pre-'67 ceasefire boundary between Israel and Jordan, always marked on maps in green. Now it is an imaginary line, the border between democratic and undemocratic Israel, the border between the ego and the id, beyond which every messianic desire is permitted, consequences notwithstanding. There is a thin green line in me too, which separates the intellect from the emotions; the latter says, let's annex Israel, let's live there; the former replies, justify youself; so the emotions weep and tell the familiar story, the intellect weakens, but rallies and reels off the reasons why we must stay put. A compromise is reached; instead of aliya we take a holiday.

7

CAESAREA

'Your shoes are great,' says Seth. I am pleased with them too. They are as red as the Med's evening sun and easily the nattiest things on a beach whose shifting sands had once borne the weight of that ancient popinjay, Herod the Great. A barefoot soccer ace, more shadow than substance, muffs a pass and the ball scoots off in our direction. I kick it back, meaning to show off my European skills to the clumsy kibbutznik, but only succeed in separating the man-made upper from the man-made sole on my Italian pump, giving me the opportunity to lecture Seth on the frailty of European civilisation and its poor record in protecting us. On the other hand (better, foot) my improvised flip-flop should be at home in Caesarea, another, more monumental, reminder of imperial brevity. Its shoreline is littered with relics of Herod's port, a city glorified with palaces pleasing to the eye, according to Flavius (not to mention the Byzantine, Crusader and Moslem settlements that followed): mosaic cubes like blind dice, marble pavements scrubbed by the sea, horizontal columns, disembodied statuary, potsherds, amber beads.

I had promised to take Seth treasure hunting, so we kneel on a shelf of the sunken harbour and excavate a hand-bored hole in the rock which formerly held a sluice gate, scooping out amid the sand five Roman coins. Once the emperors pictured thereon rose from their thrones in theatre or hippodrome and gave the thumbs down to thousands of uppity Jews; now, green-faced with bronze disease, they lie with crabs in my son's bucket. How are the mighty fallen!

The swimmers, the picnickers and the lovers begin to vacate the beach, leaving it to its ghosts. The women pull up their pants under the cover of towels or tight skirts, while the religious men, eyes averted, replace their *tzitzit* which, in this country, double as divine flak jackets. When Jonathan returned from the Lebanon he showed me the instruction manual that accompanied his American 'fragmentation protective body armor', the secular equivalent. Better American armour than European shoes, I suppose, though the former was never really tested, thank God.

Returning to our hotel we pause by the hippodrome, presently a plum orchard belonging to Kibbutz Sedot Yam, and I enter it via the Byzantine arch. I dodge the inch-long spikes on the mimosa bushes, but cannot avoid the mace-like seeds that attach themselves to my shoes. Nature hereabouts, it seems, has learnt something from the Israelis: an aggressive insistence upon propagation. We have one child, my Israeli contemporaries all aim for at least three. David Grossman (a bit younger) already has two.

We meet in Jerusalem on a Saturday and stroll up to the kibbutz at Ramat Rachel, where we sit on the grass overlooking the green and ochre hills around Bethlehem and, in the distance, the hollow mountain called Herodion, which conceals the King of Caesarea's palace. We discuss the prose of Bruno Schulz, Kafka and Anton Shammas, and why Israelis are so proud of having won the Eurovision Song Contest (because it proves they exist). Walking back down I stoop over a plant to collect some seeds for my brother who grows exotica. 'Don't,' warns David Grossman, touching one of its pods with his foot to show me why. It's round and hairy like a green

210

testicle, and on contact takes off like a bullet. 'It's called Donkey's Spit,' he says. I try to emulate him, without success. 'It took years of training,' he assures me. I look at the plant again; its flower is yellow, a five-pointed star, its leaves resemble F-111 fighters. Evolution is still at work.

Following the example of the Donkey's Spit my friends Pamela and Jonathan have Noam, Yoeli and Ma'ayan in Jerusalem; while Josanne and Arnon, her husband, have Ariel, Itamar and Michal in Herzlia Pituach. The latter, looking as elegant as a Japanese princess with her paper parasol, leads me to Tel Michal, no relation, where the Romans or their predecessors built a fort that overlooks a spectacular strip of coast, which disappears southwards into the conurbation of Tel Aviv, and northwards runs straight until it reaches the un-natural harbour of Caesarea. It has taken this long for the revolt that began there in AD 66, after a conflict between local pagans and Jews, and hit a caesura at Masada, to finally succeed and restore Jewish sovereignty to the end of the Mediterranean. I am filled with awe. My shoes, especially the broken one, are filled with sand. That's how Israel begins its seduction, at the feet, like a lover, moving by slow degrees to the knees, until passion roots you to the spot. Actually, I am already a tree in Israel, a conifer having been planted in my name at the time of my barmitzvah.

Looking inwards instead of outwards I see that a pattern is visible, meaning that a series of moves has been completed. What began with Masada has ended here, on the cliffs overlooking Caesarea, for I have taken my family to Israel, to the very place, as Joshua Sobol put it, where the Jews first brought ruin upon themselves. But will Seth ever think of this rebuilt country as home, rather than as a place for great holidays? How can I pass on my commitment? Should I send him to cheder as I was packed off by my parents? Wouldn't such a gesture be meaningless in the context of St Albans? Once Seneca's latest could have been appreciated at the theatres of Caesarea and St Albans in the same language on the same night, but not now in the babel of broken empires. Perhaps the next step is to live here. The edge of a cliff is not the best spot for such thoughts. Besides, Fran is uncertain.

8

THE MAN WHO FUCKED ISRAEL

One night, at the Pie House in Jerusalem, we have a row about it, which is a pity because the pies are tasty. Candles flicker on the tables under which attractive couples are already beginning to consummate their liaisons, also from the feet up. Perhaps Fran sees me at one of those other tables with a rival, for I have been to the Pie House without her. Does she suspect that my real life is elsewhere, in a different country, without her? But this is surely true of all writers, for we must invent our own homelands where we spend the best part of our days, utterly alone. The difference being, in this instance, that my dream country may have a correspondence in reality, may have been created for me by others. Such a view is encouraged by the presence of ancient terraces that run around the hills outside Jerusalem, physical manifestations of those imaginary contour lines you see on maps.

212

It so happens that I have a story in mind called 'The Man Who Fucked Israel', a sequel to 'The Promised Land', in which my narrator, caught with his pants down, must choose between his English wife and his Israeli mistress. Thinking that she has discovered the true source of his Zionism the wife issues the following ultimatum: Utter the word Israel just once in my presence and I'll consider us divorced. The irony being that sex, the cause of his Zionism, is no longer its mainstay. It is the crunch personified: England or Israel? 'Losing a spouse is like eating meat with horseradish,' runs a Yiddish proverb, 'you cry a little, you enjoy a little.' But it's no joke to my hero. Of course our argument is not so dramatic, nor the dilemma so clear cut. There is, in effect, a green line between the Israel of my imagination and the country itself – the Israelis in my story all converse in English – and the only way I can cross it is by changing my language. In writing my fictions I do my best to ignore its presence, as many Israelis try to ignore the green line on old maps, but neither will go away. For example: when we got off the Green Line bus at London Airport and went through all the security checks necessary before boarding an El Al jet (Said isn't the only one who has to deal with death threats), I was asked, 'Do you speak Hebrew,' and I answered, like a parrot, '*Ani lo m'daber ivrit, rak anglit,*' which means, 'I don't speak Hebrew, only English.' Perhaps my literary agent, Kissinger-like, has worked out the only compromise available: selling *Blood Libels* to an Israeli publisher, so that it will be translated into Hebrew and, once fluent, will make aliya, allowing an echo, long separated from my body and incomprehensible to me, to be heard there.

It is just before dawn and the air is indeed full of strange noises. We are standing, naked, in front of the open window, listening. Pamela and Jonathan's house, where we are staying, faces East Talpiot and, beyond that, the Old City, the Judean Hills and the Dead Sea, all of which we must take on trust, as much in the dark as the land's very first inhabitants. *Bereshis boro elohim.* Ululating out of the umbra comes a baritone, which hangs like an early-morning mist, vibrating lest the faithful forget it is time for prayers; this, in turn, is pierced by the high-pitched cough of a falcon, and soothed again by the sweet-songed leader of the dawn chorus, whose voice runs over the landscape like honey on toast, illuminating Jerusalem with a golden light. In the house opposite, now a museum dedicated to S. Y. Agnon, its former occupant, the ghost of the great writer stirs to begin another day of Hebrew prosody and I, as the spell breaks, scribble an English translation into my notebook, a permanent travelling companion, balancing every word on a thin green line. It is a moment worth preserving, a rare simulacrum of creation, when word preceded object, when shape was deduced from the presence of sound. For a few moments Israel is, literally, mine.

Later, that same afternoon, we sit on the balcony drinking mint tea with Yossel and Margaret Birstein. Fran reads some extracts from *Diaspora Blues* out loud. They seem to go down well. Yossel thinks for a few moments, then says, 'Perhaps it wouldn't be such a good thing if you came here to live, because you'd always be running back to London and we'd see less of you than we do now.' Maybe he's right. I love arriving in Israel, but in order to arrive you must first leave, which is what we are about to do.

We're spending our last night at Josanne's. I hand out bits of *Diaspora Blues*. This is the reaction of Arnon, a sabra: 'I was born here but I never learned about Zionism at school, about the French Revolution three times, but never our War of Independence. I know you want to learn about our country, so

214

tell me, why do you only meet with your friends when you come here, people who think like you do? Are you afraid that they will change your mind, or is your mind already too closed? Geula Cohen – I do not agree with her at all – but she is a brilliant woman and has a point of view. Yossi Sarid – he is an honest man though I do not agree with all his ideas – drinks coffee with her in the Knesset, rather than with his own side. Then he stands up and tears her to pieces and she does the same to him. There are giants who could fit your Joshua Sobol into their back pockets. You don't have to agree with them, but you should at least listen to them. Maybe you will say they are madmen, worse than Hitler, but how can you know if you don't listen? Things are very complex here; for example, it was under Likud, not the Marach regime, that your friends, the writers, became boldest and were given the greatest licence. It's not easy living in Israel,' he concludes, 'it's not like living in London. . . .' He's right, of course. All I can say is that this was *meant* to be a book about my friends, a book in which I have tried to convey their Israel (not to mention mine) in a language that is as lucid as possible – albeit alien to many of them. It is, I fully acknowledge, no substitute for being there, but it will do for those, like me, whose world is limited (and created) by their language.

Next morning our shoes are airborne again, and we cross the thin but fertile green line that separates Israel from the sea.

St Albans, September 1986

215